EXPERIMENTING WITH

WATER

BY ROBERT GARDNER

A VENTURE BOOK
FRANKLIN WATTS
NEW YORK/CHICAGO/LONDON/TORONTO/SYDNEY

Photographs copyright©: The Bettmann Archive: p. 12; Comstock Photography/Georg Gerster: p. 15; Robert Gardner: pp. 24, 84; Photo Researchers, Inc.: pp. 28 (Raphael Macia), 34 (National Bureau of Standards), 40 (Melissa Hayes English); Central Scientific: p. 32; Cunard Line Ltd.: p. 69; Fundamental Photographs, Inc.: pp. 81, 82 (Richard Megna); U.S. Geological Survey/A. Post: p. 118.

Library of Congress Cataloging-in-Publication Data

Gardner, Robert, 1929–
Experimenting with water / by Robert Gardner.
p. cm.—(A Venture book)
Includes bibliographical references and index.
Summary: Provides instructions for experiments and activities involving water.
ISBN 0-531-12549-1
1. Water—Experiments—Juvenile literature. [1. Water—Experiments. 2. Experiments.] I. Title
QC147.5.G37 1993   93-15586 CIP AC
546'.22—dc20

To Malcolm Skolnick, wherever you are.

CONTENTS

INTRODUCTION

If there is life elsewhere in the universe, it is most likely to be found on planets in other solar systems where water exists in the liquid state. Our explorations of Mars and Venus indicate that life in our solar system is found only on earth. Life flourishes on our globe because we are blessed with an abundance of liquid water. Although bread has been called the staff of life, water might be a better choice. There are many living organisms that survive without bread, there are even microorganisms that require no oxygen, but every living thing needs water. Water makes up two-thirds of your body weight. It comprises 90 percent of the blood that nurtures and purges your cells. It is the main ingredient of the fluid sap that carries soil nutrients to the cells of green plants. Together with carbon dioxide, water is a basic ingredient in the process of photosynthesis by which plants incorporate light energy from the sun in making the food that nourishes life.

On Mercury and Venus, temperatures are so high that any water there has vaporized. On the distant planets (Jupiter, Saturn, Uranus, Neptune, and Pluto), temperatures are so low that any water present can exist only as ice. There is evidence that water has existed on Mars and may exist now as ice beneath the surface; however, the atmosphere is so thin that any liquid that might form would quickly evaporate.

While we cannot rule out the possibility of life forms that are not water dependent, we have yet to find any. To keep our own water-dependent bodies healthy we drink, on the average, about 1.65 liters (L) of water each day, and we obtain another 0.75 L in the food we eat. The oxidation of this food provides another 0.35 L of water for our body's functions. In the same time, an equal volume of water leaves our bodies as urine (1.7 L), in feces (0.15 L), in water vapor (0.4 L) mixed with the air exhaled from our lungs, and in perspiration (0.5 L) through our skin.

In this book you'll learn, through experimentation, how water serves as a standard for various measurements. You'll learn too that while we regard water as earth's most common compound, its characteristic properties—density, freezing point, boiling point, surface tension, specific heat, heats of vaporization and fusion, and molecular structure—make it one of earth's most uncommon substances. Along the way, you'll encounter some puzzlers, which are based on your investigations. They are designed to make you think. You may want to present some of them as challenges to friends and members of your family.

The answers to the puzzlers, unlike questions raised in investigations, can be found in the back of the book. But before you turn to the answer to a puzzler, think about it for a while. Set it up and work with it if possible. You may find that you can solve the puzzler on your own. Turn to the back of the book only as a last resort.

SAFETY FIRST

Some of the tools and procedures used in science can be dangerous if you are careless or haven't been trained to use a particular piece of equipment. **I've tried to alert you to any potential danger or procedure that requires caution by using bold type.** In a few places, for reasons of safety, I've indicated that you should ask an adult to help you. In anything that you do, keep in mind the following rules about safety.

SAFETY RULES

1. Read all instructions carefully before proceeding with an experiment.
2. Maintain a serious attitude while experimenting. Fooling around can be dangerous to you and to others.
3. Wear safety goggles when you are experimenting or are in a laboratory setting. Wear a lab apron if you are working with chemicals.
4. Do not eat or drink while experimenting and do not taste dry chemicals or solutions. In many experiments you will be using alcohol, which is a poisonous and flammable liquid.
5. Keep flammable materials, such as alcohol, away from sources of heat.

---

6. Have safety equipment such as fire extinguishers, fire blankets, and a first-aid kit nearby while you are experimenting and know where this equipment is.

7. Don't touch glass that has recently been heated; it looks the same as cool glass. Bathe skin burns in cold water or apply ice.

8. Never experiment with household electricity without the supervision of a knowledgeable adult, and never put your fingers or any object other than an electrical plug into an electrical outlet.

THE
WORLD'S FOREVER MOVING WATER

The world contains 1,370,000,000 cubic kilometers (328,000,000 cubic miles) of water. As you might guess, most of the world's water—97 percent—is found in the oceans. Another 37,500,000 cubic kilometers (9,000,000 cubic miles) is frozen in the earth's polar caps. Table 1 reveals that less than 1 percent of the world's water is available for human use.

Underground water is found in aquifers that lie mostly beneath the earth's surface. They were formed and are replenished by rainwater seeping through the soil to saturate the spaces between porous rock and gravel that rest on impermeable bedrock. In any given area, the top of this saturated space is the water table. Sometimes aquifers are stacked one above another separated by impervious soil or rock as shown in Figure 1.

Wells, from which water can be pumped, are made by drilling into aquifers. Some aquifers are so deep that their water is heated by the earth's hot inner core.

More than two-thirds of the earth's surface is covered by water.

TABLE 1: Where the World's Water Is Located.

Where	Amount in Cubic Kilometers (cubic miles in parentheses)
Oceans	1,320,000,000 (317,000,000)
Polar caps	37,530,000 (9,000,000)
Underground (available)	4,170,000 (1,000,000)
Underground (unavailable)	4,170,000 (1,000,000)
Lakes and ponds	125,000 (30,000)
Soil	66,700 (16,000)
Atmosphere	12,900 (3,100)
Rivers	1250 (300)

If such aquifers have openings that reach the earth's surface, they may provide hot springs or steam generated geysers. Cold-water springs may be found in shallower aquifers where their water tables reach ground level (Figure 1). Other aquifers may discharge into rivers, most, but not all, of which empty into the sea.

Puzzler 1: All the World's Water

If all the world's water were to be placed in a single cubic vessel, what would be the length of one side of the cube?

THE WATER CYCLE

Water flowing along rivers and ocean currents is visible evidence that the world's water is moving. The movement of water is less apparent in lakes, ponds, and aquifers; however, chemical tracers reveal that this water is also in motion. And the invisible process of evaporation constantly brings water into the earth's

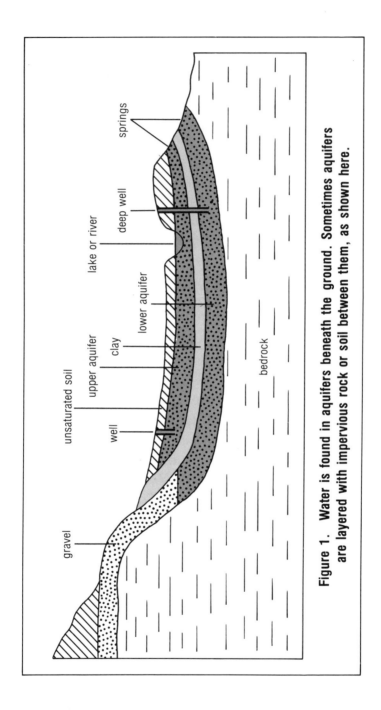

Figure 1. Water is found in aquifers beneath the ground. Sometimes aquifers are layered with impervious rock or soil between them, as shown here.

Groundwater heated by proximity to molten rock will produce geysers such as these in Yellowstone National Park in Wyoming.

atmosphere, where 12,900 cubic kilometers (3100 cubic miles) of water exist in the gaseous state (see Table 1).

Figure 2 shows that 509,000 cubic kilometers (122,000 cubic miles) of water evaporates each year, mostly from the surface of the oceans. An equal amount condenses annually and falls as rain. About one-quarter of the rain falls on land and flows along rivers. A close look at Figure 2 reveals that 41,700 more cubic kilometers (10,000 cubic miles) of water evaporates from the ocean annually than falls into it as rain. This excess volume falls as rain on the continents. Much of this water flows over and through the land back to the sea. The distribution of the 5.8 cubic kilometers (1.4 cubic miles or 1.5 trillion gallons) of water that falls as rain on the continental United States each year is shown in Figure 3.

Investigation 1: Dew Point

MATERIALS NEEDED
• Shiny metal can • Thermometer • Ice • Warm water

The amount of gaseous water that can be found in a volume of air depends on the temperature of the air. Table 2 indicates that the warmer the air, the more water vapor it can hold.

Unless it is raining, the amount of moisture in the air is usually less than the maximum it can hold. The dampness of air can be measured by the *absolute humidity*—the quantity of water vapor in 1 cubic meter (m^3) of air. The absolute humidity is determined by finding the dew point—the temperature at which dew

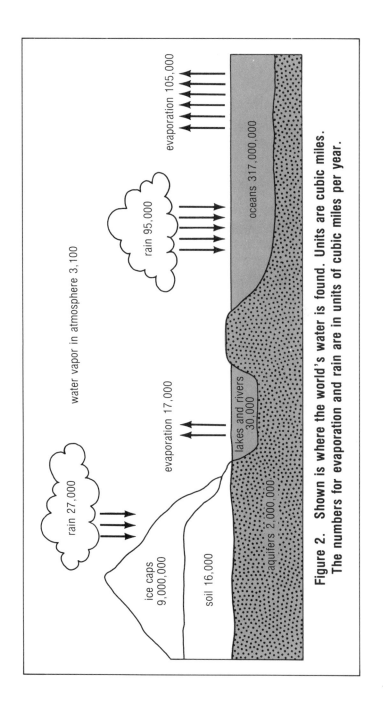

Figure 2.   Shown is where the world's water is found. Units are cubic miles.
The numbers for evaporation and rain are in units of cubic miles per year.

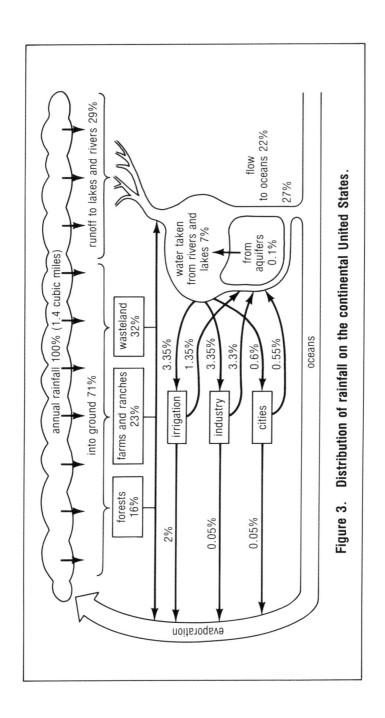

Figure 3. Distribution of rainfall on the continental United States.

TABLE 2: The Maximum Amount of Water Vapor in a Cubic Meter of Air at Different Temperatures.	
Temperature (°C)	Water Vapor (g/m^3)
0	4.8
5	6.8
10	9.3
15	12.7
20	17.1
25	22.8
30	30.0
35	39.2

begins to form. For example, if the temperature of the air is 20°C (68°F), it can hold a maximum of 17.1 g/m^3 (Table 2); however, it probably holds less than this maximum amount. If you pour some warm water into a shiny metal can and slowly lower its temperature, you can observe the temperature at which dew begins to form on the outside of the can. Moisture will begin to form on the can when the air in contact with it reaches the temperature at which the air is saturated with water vapor. If dew droplets appear when the water and can reach a temperature of 10°C (50°F), we know the air holds 9.3 g/m^3—the saturation point for water in air at this temperature. Since the air not in contact with the can is at 20°C, it is not saturated with water; it could hold as much as 17.1 g/m^3.

The absolute humidity of this air would be 9.3 g/m^3. The *relative humidity* is the ratio of the quantity of water vapor the air *does* hold to the quantity it *could* hold if it were saturated with moisture. In this case, the relative humidity of the air is 9.3/17.1 or 54 percent.

To find the absolute humidity of the air in your home or school, pour some warm water into a shiny can. Stir the water carefully with a thermometer as you lower the water temperature by adding small pieces of ice. Watch the surface of the can carefully. When the surface first becomes clouded with dew, note the temperature. You have reached the dew point.

Use your experimental data and Table 2 to determine the absolute humidity of the air. A graph of absolute humidity versus temperature will help you to determine values for temperatures not given in the table. What is the relative humidity? How does the humidity outside the building compare with the humidity inside?

Use the same apparatus, table, and graph to determine the dew point and humidity on clear, cloudy, and rainy days, and at different times of the year. During which season of the year does the absolute humidity tend to be highest? Lowest? When is the relative humidity highest? Lowest? During which season of the year is the air driest inside your home or school?

WATER: A COMMON LIQUID WITH UNCOMMON PROPERTIES

Although water is the most common liquid in the world, it has a number of uncommon properties. Unlike most liquids, it expands when it freezes and is most compact (dense) not at or below its freezing point but at a temperature 4°C above its freezing point. Its molecules, which consist of two atoms of hydrogen bonded to one atom of oxygen (the familiar H_2O), are polar. Electrical charges are not evenly distributed in polar

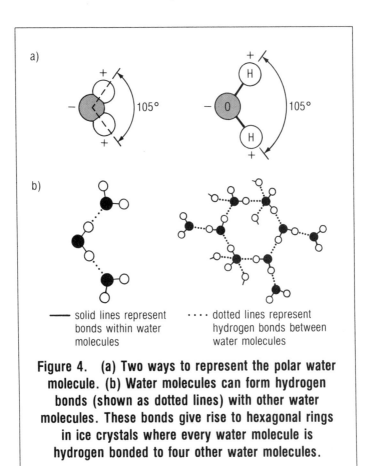

Figure 4. (a) Two ways to represent the polar water molecule. (b) Water molecules can form hydrogen bonds (shown as dotted lines) with other water molecules. These bonds give rise to hexagonal rings in ice crystals where every water molecule is hydrogen bonded to four other water molecules.

molecules. Consequently, one side of a water molecule has a slight positive charge, the other a slight negative charge. Figure 4*a* shows that water molecules are not linear. The angle between the hydrogen atoms in the molecule is about 105°. Because the oxygen atom attracts electrons more strongly than do the hydrogen atoms, the oxygen side of the molecule is slightly negative; the hydrogen side is slightly positive.

The positive ends of the polar molecules of water form weak chemical bonds with the negative ends of other polar molecules including other water molecules (Figure 4b). It is these bonds, called hydrogen bonds, that give rise to the crystalline structure of ice. The polarity of water molecules makes water a suitable liquid (solvent) for dissolving polar molecules and the ions (charged atoms) of a great many salts. Because of the strong attraction of water molecules for one another, water melts and boils at temperatures well above the melting and boiling temperatures of many much heavier molecules.

Investigation 2: Water Molecules in an Electric Field

Materials Needed

• Plastic comb or ruler • Paper or cloth • Water tap • Silk cloth and glass rod or test tube • Rubber or amber rod and wool or fur

An electric field surrounds any electrically charged object. Two such fields, represented by imaginary lines that show the direction of the force on positive units of charge, are shown in Figure 5.

If, in a dry room (low humidity), you rub a plastic comb or ruler with a piece of paper or a cloth, the plastic will acquire a charge. What happens when you hold the charged comb or ruler near an extremely thin stream of water flowing from a faucet? How can you explain what you observed?

Do you think the charge on the comb or ruler—positive or negative—will affect the direction of the force on the polar molecules in the stream of water? To find out, you can do what Benjamin Franklin did when he first defined the sign on electric charges. Use,

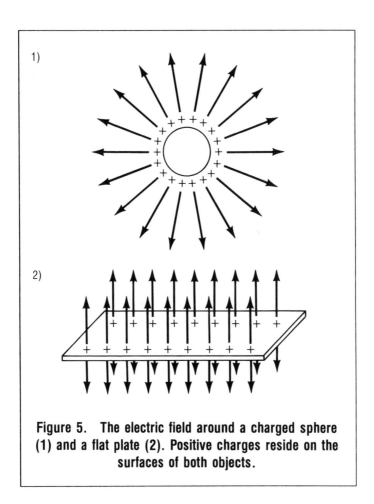

Figure 5. The electric field around a charged sphere (1) and a flat plate (2). Positive charges reside on the surfaces of both objects.

as he did, a silk cloth to rub a glass rod or test tube. Franklin defined the charge acquired by the glass to be positive. Similarly, the charge acquired by a rubber or amber rod rubbed with wool or fur is said to be negative because it attracts the charged glass. If you don't have these materials, you can probably borrow them from your school.

Does a positively charged glass rod attract or repel

**Perform Investigation 2 to detect the polarity
of water molecules in an electric field.**

the water molecules in a thin stream of water? How about a negatively charged rod? How can you explain the results of your experiment?

WATER AND LIFE

Water is essential to life, as is food. Green plants, the only living organisms that can manufacture food from natural compounds, combine water and carbon dioxide to make food in a process called photosynthesis. The *synthesis* part of the word comes from the fact that the food is made by combining simpler substances. The *photo* part of the word indicates that the process takes place only when sunlight is present to provide the energy needed in the reaction or synthesis. Chlorophyll, the green pigment that gives these plants their color, catalyzes or speeds up the process.

The bulk of the living tissue found in the cells of both plants and animals is water. At birth, the human body is 78 percent water; however, that fraction gradually decreases to about 60 percent with age. Within the body, blood is 90 percent water, muscles are 75 percent water, two-thirds of the liver is water, and even our ''dry'' bones are 22 percent water.

Investigation 3: Percentage of Water in Foods

MATERIALS NEEDED
- Hot toast and plate • Balance • Bread and other foods such as apple, potato, carrot, banana, and meat • Small aluminum pans • Oven

What fraction of the various foods we eat is water? To find out, you can weigh food before and after it is dried. The food can be dried by placing it in a warm oven. To see that water is removed from food when it is heated, place a slice of hot toast on a cold plate. After a minute or so lift the toast from the plate. What do you see on the plate?

To determine the fraction of bread that is water, use a balance to weigh a small aluminum pan. Then place a slice of fresh bread on the pan and weigh again. How much does the bread weigh? Place pan and bread in a warm (150°F) oven for 2 hours. Then weigh the bread again. How much water did the bread lose?

Place the bread back in the oven for a few minutes before you weigh it again. Continue heating and weighing until the bread is thoroughly dry and its weight does not decrease any further. What fraction of the bread's original weight was water?

Try the same experiment with a number of different foods such as slices of apple, potato, carrot, banana, and meat. To save time, you can place each sample in separate containers, weigh them, and put them all in a warm oven at the same time. Which food seems to contain the largest percentage of water? The least percentage of water?

- How can you find out whether dry seeds contain water?

WHERE DOES YOUR DRINKING WATER COME FROM? WHERE DOES IT GO?

You turn on a faucet and water emerges. But how did it get there? The source of your tap water depends on where you live. Most rural homes obtain their water from a well or spring, but urban and many suburban dwellings share a common water source. If you live in a major city, your water probably comes from huge reservoirs. Smaller cities and towns may rely on a large river, lake, or wells drilled into an aquifer.

Investigation 4: Your Source of Water

To find out where the water in your home or school comes from, ask your parents or teacher for permission to follow the path of the pipes that carry water to and from your water taps. You can begin beneath a sink by finding the pipes that lead to the hot and cold water taps. You'll also find a larger pipe that is probably located between the two pipes that lead to the faucets. What is the purpose of the larger pipe? Where is it connected to the sink? Where is its other end?

Trace the hot- and cold-water pipes. Where do they end? If they enter walls, ask a friend to help you by tapping on the pipes while you listen in the basement or wherever you think the pipes may lead. Where and how is the hot water heated? Do the hot and cold water pipes have a common origin? Make a drawing of the way water is distributed in your home.

Once you have located the place where water enters the building, see whether you can find out where the water comes from. Does it come from a well? A reservoir? A river? How is the water moved from its origin to the building? Is the water treated in any way before or after it enters your home? For example, is

Many cities obtain their water from large reservoirs.
The Croton Reservoir supplies water to New York City.

it chlorinated? Is it fluorinated? Softened? Are there settling basins? If so, what happens in these basins? Is the water filtered?

Investigation 5: How Much Water Do You Use?

MATERIALS NEEDED

- Yardstick or ruler • Stopwatch or watch with second hand or mode
- Measuring container such as 1-gallon container or plastic pail with gallon markings

Once you know where your water comes from and how it is distributed, you might like to figure out how much water is used in your home each day. You'll be surprised by the amount your family uses in a single day. If you have a water meter, it's very easy to find out how much you use.

Whether you have a meter or not, you can find out how water is used in your home. One of the major water uses is for toilets. In older toilets each flush requires about 5 gallons of water. You can find the volume of water in a toilet tank by measuring the length, width, and depth of water in the tank with a yardstick or ruler. You'll also need to know that 1 gallon of water occupies 3.79 liters (4 quarts or 231 cubic inches).

In a similar way, you can measure the water required to take a bath or wash clothes. To find the water used in taking a shower, watering the lawn, washing the car, brushing teeth, washing or rinsing dishes, and so on, you'll have to collect the water over a period of half a minute or a minute in a measuring container and then use a watch or clock to measure the time the water is used for each activity. If you have a dishwasher, check the manual to see how much water it uses. (Most require about 15 gallons per wash.)

How much water is used in your household each day? Does it vary much from day to day? Of the various water uses in your home, which one consumes the most water? What percentage of the water is used for flushing toilets? Washing dishes and clothes? Bathing or showering? Cooking? Brushing teeth? Other water-using activities?

On the average, Americans use 60 gallons of water per day per person. Twenty-seven gallons (45 percent) is used for flushing toilets, 18 gallons (30 percent) for bathing, 6 gallons (10 percent) for laundry, the same amount for outdoor use, and 3 gallons (5 percent) for cooking and preparing food. How do your totals and percentages compare with the averages given here?

A century ago the average person used less than 10 percent of the water used today. Make a list of the factors that have increased our water use by more than ten times in the last hundred years.

Water is our most valuable resource and many areas of the country experience frequent or constant water shortages. Ask your family members to think of various ways in which they can reduce the use of water in your home. For example, a 3-minute shower requires much less water than a bath, devices are available that reduce the volume of water in toilet tanks, washing clothes and dishes might be done only when there are full loads, and so on. Then encourage your family to carry out these measures.

C H A P T E R   T W O

WATER:
A STANDARD
FOR
MEASURING

Because water is such a common liquid it has served as a standard for a variety of measurements. After the French Revolution, French scientists made an attempt to develop a completely logical system of measurement based on decimals. It is known as the metric system, and its fundamental unit of length is the meter. The meter was chosen to be one-ten millionth of the distance from the North Pole to the equator. The unit of time was the second, which they chose to be equal to 1/100,000 of a day. The kilogram, which was chosen as the standard unit of mass, was equal to the mass of 1 cubic decimeter (1000 cm^3, 0.001 m^3 or 1.0 liter) of water.

The meter is still very nearly 1/10,000,000 the distance from the North Pole to the equator. Millions of clock owners, however, rejected the idea of having to buy new clocks and so the second reverted to its former value of 1/86,400th of a day. Despite its logic,

A cubic box such as this one that measures
10 cm on a side will hold exactly 1.0 L (1,000 cubic
centimeters) of water with a mass of 1 kilogram.

the idea of a 10-hour day, with 100-minute-long hours and 100-second-long minutes, never caught on.

Because water is such a common liquid, the founders of the metric system believed that the standard mass could be duplicated anywhere in the world. As techniques of measurement became more refined, it was realized that such factors as evaporation and inaccuracies in measuring volume made the standard less than ideal. Consequently, the present standard for the kilogram is a cylinder of platinum alloy that is kept at Sèvres, France. It can be used to balance other masses, which can be adjusted to equal the standard and then sent to laboratories throughout the world. For most practical purposes, however, the original definition of mass based on a volume of water is a reasonable and practical one.

BEYOND MKS

The metric system is often referred to as the mks system because of its units—*m*eters (m), *k*ilograms (kg), and *s*econds (s). It also has smaller units, called the cgs system, which are sometimes more practical. These units are *c*entimeters (cm), *g*rams (g), and *s*econds(s). A centimeter is 0.01 m and a gram is 0.001 kg.

Just as a kilogram is the mass of 1.0 L of water, so the gram is the mass of 1 cubic centimeter (cm^3) or 1 milliliter (mL) of water. A cm^3 has the same volume as a mL, which is 0.001 L.

Mass is not the only measurement for which water serves as a practical standard. The *specific gravity* of a substance is defined as the ratio of its mass to the mass

This platinum-iridium cylinder at the National Bureau of Standards in Washington, D.C., is the primary standard kilogram for all metric measurements of mass in this country. It is 39 mm in diameter and 39 mm high.

of an equal volume of water. The melting and boiling points of water serve as standard calibration points for thermometers and are used to define temperatures. Heat may be measured in units called calories, Calories, joules, or British thermal units (Btu's). A calorie (cal) is the amount of heat needed to raise the temperature of 1 g of *water* through 1 degree Celsius (1°C). A Calorie is the amount of heat required to raise the temperature of 1 kg of *water* through 1°C. A joule (J) of heat is the amount of heat required to raise the temperature of 0.24 g of *water* through 1°C. (Thus, $1.0 J = 0.24 cal$.) A Btu is the amount of heat required to raise the temperature of 1 pound of *water* through 1 degree Fahrenheit (1°F).

The specific heat of a substance is the amount of heat required to raise the temperature of 1 g of the substance through 1°C. The specific heats of a variety of substances can be found by noting their temperature changes when they are supplied with the same amount of heat as an equal mass of water. The specific heat of water is 1 calorie per gram per degree Celsius (1 cal/g/°C or 1 cal/g · °C).

The acidity or alkalinity of chemical substances is measured in terms of a pH scale with a range of 1 to 14. The center of the scale—pH 7—is the pH of pure water, which is neutral. Substances that are more acidic than water have a pH less than 7; substances less acidic than water have a pH greater than 7.

Water is often called the universal solvent because so many substances dissolve in it. In fact one of the properties used to identify a substance is its solubility in water at various temperatures. Solubility is measured in grams of solute (the stuff that dissolves) per gram, or per 100 grams, of water (the solvent).

In the next several investigations you'll examine some of these measurements in which water serves as a standard. In later chapters you'll see that water can serve as a standard for measuring a variety of other properties as well—surface tension (a liquid's internal "grabbiness" or tendency to hold together), vaporization, pressure, and so on.

Investigation 6: Density and Specific Gravity, Where Water Is 1.0

MATERIALS NEEDED
- Graduated cylinder, 100-mL • Laboratory balance • Cold water
- Liquid soap or detergent • Isopropyl or rubbing alcohol; **caution!**: both are **flammable and poisonous** • Cooking oil

The density of a substance is defined as its mass per unit volume. To find the density of water simply determine the mass of a 100-mL graduated cylinder using a laboratory balance. Then fill the cylinder to the 100-mL line with cold water. The bottom of the meniscus (the curved surface of the water) should be on the 100-mL line. Reweigh the cylinder and subtract its dry mass from the mass of the water and cylinder. What is the mass of 100 mL of water? To find the density of water divide the mass of the sample weighed by its volume. What is the density of water in grams per milliliter (g/mL)? In grams per cubic centimeter (g/cm^3)? Why is it better to find the density of a substance by measuring the mass of a large volume rather than the mass of a small volume such as 1 mL?

Predict the mass of 50 mL of water. Of 200 mL of water. Then test your predictions. Were you right?

Determine the density of alcohol. **Work under adult supervision. Remember that alcohol is flammable and poisonous! Extinguish any flames** that may be nearby before pouring alcohol. Is it more or less dense than water?

Make a soapy water solution by adding a few drops of liquid soap or detergent to some water. Watch the level of the water, and thereby its volume, as you add the soap. (Ignore any bubbles.) Do you think adding the soap changed the density of the water significantly? Check up on your guess by finding the density of the soapy water. Did the density of the water change very much when the soap was added?

What is the density of cooking oil?

Remembering that the specific gravity of a substance is defined as the ratio of its mass to the mass of an equal volume of water, what is the specific gravity of alcohol? Of soapy water? Of cooking oil?

- Using what you have learned, find the density and specific gravity of some different metals. If one or more of the metals do not have a regular shape, how can you find their volumes?

Investigation 7: Water and Thermometers

MATERIALS NEEDED

- Laboratory thermometer, 10°–110°C • Masking tape • Small (pint or half-pint) plastic container • Ice chips or shavings, or snow • Pencil or pen • Stove and teakettle • Ruler

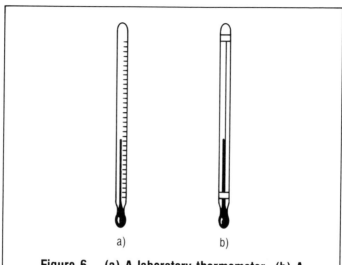

Figure 6. (a) A laboratory thermometer. (b) A laboratory thermometer that has its scale covered with masking tape.

Earlier in this chapter you read that water is used in calibrating thermometers. To see how this is done, you'll need a laboratory thermometer similar to the one shown in Figure 6, which has a scale from $-10°$ to $110°C$. Use a narrow strip of masking tape to cover the scale on the thermometer. You now have a thermometer without a scale.

Fill a small container with ice chips, ice shavings, or snow. Add a little cold water to make a slush of melting ice or snow. Put the thermometer into the cold slush and stir carefully until the liquid in the thermometer stops contracting. Then use a pencil or pen to mark the level of the liquid on the tape. Your thermometer now has one temperature point on it—the melting point of ice (solid water). Do you think this point will change if you add more ice or snow to the cold mixture? Try it! Were you right?

The point on your thermometer, which corresponds to the melting point of ice, can be labeled 0, which is the number Celsius chose, or 32, which is the number Fahrenheit chose, or any other number you choose to use. The point is that the choice is arbitrary. But to make a scale, you need a second point. You might choose the temperature of the human body as some early scientists did, or the lowest level of the liquid that can be obtained when ice and salt are mixed, which was the point some other scientists chose. The other commonly accepted point today is the temperature of boiling water at sea level. Sea level (actually a barometric pressure of 76 cm of mercury) is chosen as standard pressure because boiling points change with altitude because air pressure decreases as we ascend into the atmosphere.

To find the boiling point on your thermometer, you should **work under adult supervision and wear safety goggles and gloves**. Pour some water into a teakettle and bring it to a boil on a stove or hot plate. Carefully insert the bulb end of the thermometer into the spout of the teakettle so that it is in the steam above the boiling water. Notice what happens to the liquid in your thermometer. When the liquid level in the thermometer finally stops rising, make a second mark on the tape attached to the thermometer at the new level of the liquid. Remove the thermometer from the steam and turn off the stove or hot plate. What happens to the liquid in the thermometer when it is removed from the steam?

What happens to the air pressure as you ascend in the atmosphere?

With the melting and boiling points of water on the tape, you can devise a thermometer scale. Simply divide the distance between the marks into a convenient number of divisions. Again, any number could be chosen for the boiling point. One scale, established by Celsius, is to call the melting point of water 0° and the boiling point 100°.

Mark the two points on your thermometer 0 and 100 so that you can make a Celsius scale. Use a ruler to divide the distance between the two points into degrees. To save time, mark only 10-degree intervals. How can you extend the scale to include temperatures above 100° and below 0°?

Now put your thermometer to work. Use it to make an estimate of the temperature of the room you are in. Place the thermometer under your armpit. Keep it in place by holding your arm firmly against your body. After a couple of minutes, remove the thermometer. What is your body temperature in degrees Celsius according to your thermometer?

Carefully remove the tape with your scale on it from the thermometer. How closely does your scale agree with the one that was on it?

- Are the melting point of ice and the freezing point of water the same? Design and carry out an experiment to find out.

Puzzler 2: Freezing and Boiling Points on Other Temperature Scales
What are some other common temperature scales besides the Celsius scale? What are the melting and boiling points of water on these scales?

Investigation 8: Water, Heat, and Calories

MATERIALS NEEDED
- Celsius thermometer(s), two that are identical, if possible
- Ice water (about 0°C) and hot tap water (about 40°C)
- Foam plastic cups—12- or 14-oz and 6- or 7-oz • Pitchers
- Graduated cylinder, 100-mL

As you read earlier, heat is usually measured in units of calories, Calories, joules, or Btu's. All these units are based on the amount of heat needed to raise the temperature of a certain mass of water by 1 degree.

Now, let's make an assumption. Let's assume that if a gram of water gains 1 calorie of heat when its temperature rises 1 degree, then it will lose 1 calorie when its temperature drops 1 degree. To test that assumption you can mix hot and cold water in insulated containers and measure the temperature changes of both the hot and the cold water. It will be useful to have a partner to help you with these experiments.

If possible, find two thermometers that read very nearly the same when placed in the same container of water. (If you have only one thermometer, you can measure the temperature of the cold water and then cover it with an inverted insulated cup while you measure the temperature of the hot water.) Prepare a pitcher of ice water by mixing ice cubes and cold water. You'll also need a pitcher of hot tap water. Measure out 100 g (100 mL) of ice water with the graduated cylinder and pour it into one of the small insulated cups. Make sure there is no ice in the ice water. Do the same with 100 g of hot (40°–50°C) tap water. Place a thermometer in both samples of water. Just before you mix the hot and cold water, you should read the temperature of the cold water while your partner reads the temperature of the hot water. Then quickly pour both the hot and the cold water into the large insulated cup. Stir the water and read the final temperature of the mixture.

Now you have some data to test the assumption we made earlier. How much heat did the cold water gain? Suppose its temperature was 4°C before it was mixed and the temperature of the mixture is 22°C. The

100 g of cold water must have gained 1800 cal of heat because

$$100 \text{ g} \times (22°C - 4°C) = 1800 \text{ cal.}$$

Since we have defined the specific heat, S, of water to be 1.0 cal/g°C, it would be more proper to write the preceding equation with the specific heat included:

$$100 \text{ g}(22°C - 4°C)(1 \text{ cal/g} \cdot °C) = 1800 \text{ cal.}$$

In this way the units on both sides of the equation agree because

$$\text{g} \times °C \times \frac{\text{cal}}{\text{g} \times °C} = \text{cal.}$$

The heat to warm the cold water must have come from the hot water. If the temperature of the 100 g of hot water dropped by about 18°C, then we have good evidence for believing that our assumption was correct. Do your results confirm the assumption we made? Can you confirm our assumption by using unequal masses of hot and cold water? For example, what happens if you mix 150 g of cold water with 75 g of hot water? Or 75 g of cold water with 150 g of hot water?

Investigation 9: Water, Heat, and Specific Heat

MATERIALS NEEDED
- 100-mL Graduated cylinder • Cooking oil • Water
- Plastic foam cups—12- or 14-oz and 6- or 7-oz • Refrigerator
- Two thermometers (− 10°C–0°C), identical if possible

As you probably found in the previous investigation, the heat that 1 gram of hot water loses when it cools 1 degree is equal to the heat that 1 gram of cold water gains when its temperature rises 1 degree. The experiment you performed was also one among thousands that confirm the law of conservation of energy. In your experiment the heat transferred *from* the hot water equals the heat transferred *to* the cold water.

Most substances cannot absorb as much heat per degree as water can; that is, it takes less than 1 calorie to raise the temperature of most substances by 1°C. You can see this for yourself by mixing 100 g of hot tap water with 100 g of cold cooking oil. From another experiment, you know that the density of cooking oil is less than that of water. In fact, the density of the oil is about 0.90 g/mL. Consequently, you'll need to measure out about 110 mL of cooking oil in order to obtain 100 g of the substance because

$$\frac{100 \text{ g}}{0.90 \text{ g/mL}} = 110 \text{ mL}.$$

Use a graduated cylinder to measure out 110 mL of cooking oil. Pour the oil into a small plastic foam cup and place it in a refrigerator for several hours. When the oil has cooled, pour 100 g (100 mL) of hot tap water into a second small insulated cup. Have a partner help you record the temperatures of both liquids—at the same time if possible. Then pour both liquids into a large insulated cup. Stir thoroughly and record the final temperature of the mixture. Which liquid showed the larger temperature change? How much heat, in calories, did the hot water lose? Assuming conservation of energy, how much heat did the cooking oil gain?

Does oil require more or less heat to change 1 degree than an equal mass of water?

From the data you obtained when you mixed cold cooking oil and hot water, you can determine the specific heat of cooking oil. Suppose that the temperatures of the water and the oil just before you mix them are 40°C and 5°C, respectively. If the temperature after they are mixed is 28°C, the water must have transferred 1200 cal to the cold cooking oil because

$$100 \text{ g}(40°C - 28°C)(1.0 \text{ cal/g} \cdot °C) = 1200 \text{ cal.}$$

The heat from the water warmed the 100 g of cooking oil from 5°C to 28°C. We don't know the specific heat of cooking oil, but we do know that 1200 cals of heat was needed to raise the temperature of 100 g of the oil from 5°C to 28°C. Therefore, we can calculate the specific heat, S, from the data. Since

$$100 \text{ g} \times (28°C - 5°C) \times S_{oil} = 1200 \text{ cal.}$$

$$S_{oil} = \frac{1200 \text{ cal}}{100 \text{ g} \times 23°C} = 0.52 \text{ cal/g} \cdot °C.$$

From your data, what value do you find for the specific heat of cooking oil?

Investigation 10: Another Way to Find the Specific Heat of Cooking Oil

MATERIALS NEEDED
- 100-mL Graduated cylinder • Cold water • Cooking oil
- Plastic foam cups—6- or 7-oz • Refrigerator

- Thermometer (-10–$50°C$) • Electric immersion heater, 200-watt
- Clock or watch with second hand or second mode

You could find the specific heat of cooking oil by comparing the temperature changes of water and cooking oil when both receive the same amount of heat. The heat can be supplied by an immersion heater like the kind used to make a cup of tea or coffee. **Because you'll be using household electricity in this experiment, you should work under adult supervision**. You should also remember that **an immersion heater should never be connected to an electrical outlet unless it is immersed in a liquid!**

Use a graduated cylinder to measure out 100 g (100 mL) of cold water and 100 g (110 mL) of cooking oil. Pour each liquid into separate small foam plastic cups. Place the cups in a refrigerator for about half an hour. When the liquids are cool, remove them from the refrigerator. Place the immersion heater in the water, but **don't plug it in** yet. Use a thermometer to find the initial temperature of the water. Note the time. Then plug the heater into an electrical outlet for exactly 30 seconds. While the water is being heated, stir it gently with the heater. After 30 seconds, disconnect the heater by pulling its plug, **not its cord. Do not remove the heater from the water.** The heater is still warm and you want all of its heat to be transferred to the water. Stir the water with the thermometer and record the final temperature of the water. How much heat did the heater transfer to the water in 30 seconds?

Repeat the experiment with the 100 g of cold cooking oil. Be sure to stir constantly with the heater throughout the 30 seconds you heat the liquid. **Don't**

46

let the heater touch the sides of the cup. (Oil does not conduct heat as well as water and the heater could melt the wall of the cup.) After disconnecting the heater, use it to stir the liquid. What is the final temperature of the cooking oil?

To find the specific heat of the cooking oil, you can assume that the heater transferred the same amount of heat to the oil as it did to the water during the 30 seconds that it was connected. For example, if the heater warmed the water from 10°C to 25°C, then it provided 1500 cal of heat in the 30 seconds it was operating. It's reasonable to assume that in 30 seconds it would provide 1500 cal to the cooking oil as well. If the temperature of the cooking oil rose from 5°C to 35°C, then we can use that data to calculate its specific heat, S_{oil}:

$$100 \text{ g}(35°C - 5°C)(S_{oil}) = 1500 \text{ cal}$$

$$S_{oil} = \frac{1500 \text{ cal}}{100 \text{ g} \times 30°C} = 0.50 \text{ cal/g} \cdot °C.$$

What do you find the specific heat of cooking oil to be using this method? How does it compare with the value you found by mixing hot water and cold cooking oil? Why might the values not be identical?

- **Under adult supervision,** use the immersion heater method to find the specific heat of ethylene glycol (automobile antifreeze).
- Design an experiment to find the specific heat of some common metals such as copper, iron, lead, and zinc. Then, **under adult supervision,** carry out the experiment you've designed.

Investigation 11: Acids, Bases, Water, and pH

MATERIALS NEEDED

- Paper, pH (1 to 4) • Eyedropper • Vinegar, lemon juice, coffee, tea, milk, rainwater, and tap water • Household ammonia • Baking soda, salt, and sugar • Small container • Stirrer, spoon, straw, or coffee stick

Acids are substances that have a sour taste, react with some metals such as zinc to form hydrogen, conduct electric current, and form hydrogen at the negative electrode when they undergo electrolysis. They cause color changes in certain plant dyes called acid-base indicators; for example, they change the color of litmus from blue to red. They also react with bases to form salts and water. Bases, on the other hand, have a bitter taste and feel slippery. They have the opposite effect of acids on some plant dyes. For example, they turn litmus from red to blue. Bases react with acids to form salts, and, like acids, they conduct electricity.

Because acids react with certain metals to form hydrogen, conduct electric current, and release hydrogen at the negative electrode during electrolysis, chemists concluded that solutions of acids contain hydrogen ions (H^+). Since bases conduct electric current and combine with acids to form water, which is known to have the formula H_2O or HOH, chemists had reason to believe that basic solutions contain hydroxide ions (OH^-). When an acid and a base react, they are said to neutralize each other because they combine to form water. The reaction may be represented by the following ionic equation:

$$H^+ + OH^- \rightarrow H_2O.$$

If we take into account the ions that are combined with H^+ ions in the acid and OH^- ions in the base, then you can see why salts are also formed when acids and bases combine. For example, hydrochloric acid (HCl) forms H^+ and Cl^- ions in solution. Sodium hydroxide contains Na^+ ions and OH^- ions in solution. The reaction between the ions of hydrochloric acid and sodium hydroxide may be written:

$$H^+ + Cl^- + Na^+ + OH^- \rightarrow Na^+Cl^- + H_2O.$$

The strength of an acid or basic solution is measured by its pH, which is related to the concentration of H^+ ions in the solution. A pH of 1 indicates that a solution is strongly acidic, a pH of 14 indicates a strong basic solution, and a pH of 7 indicates a neutral solution— one where the H^+ and OH^- ions are equal and small in number because most of them have combined to form pure water.

You can use pH paper to measure the pH of a solution. The paper is made by combining a number of acid-base indicators (plant dyes). When a drop of solution is placed on the pH paper, the color of the paper can be matched with one of the standard colors on the paper's container. These standard colors indicate the pH of the solution.

Use pH paper and an eyedropper to determine the pH of a number of different liquids. Be sure to rinse the eyedropper after each use. You might try some of the following liquids: vinegar, lemon juice, coffee, tea, milk, rainwater, and tap water. Which of these are acids? Which are bases? Which are neutral? Were you surprised by the pH of water and rainwater? How can you explain the pH of these water samples?

Ask an adult to help you dilute a household ammonia solution by adding a few drops of the ammonia to about the same volume of cold water. What is the pH of ammonia? Is it an acid or a base?

You might also test solutions of baking soda, salt, and sugar. Each solid can be dissolved by adding it to water in a small container and stirring to dissolve. Which of these solutions are acids? Bases? Neutral?

Investigation 12: Solubility and Water

MATERIALS NEEDED

- Teaspoon • Sugar • Glass • Water • Corn starch or flour
- Methanol (**poisonous**) • Small jars or test tubes • Moth flakes (**poisonous**) • Kosher salt (sodium chloride) • Graduated cylinder
- Small bottle or a large test tube • Balance • Tea cup or evaporating dish • Sodium nitrate (if possible)

One of the properties used to identify a substance is its solubility in water or other liquids. For example, add a teaspoonful of sugar to a glass of warm water and stir. The fact that the sugar disappears after you stir it indicates that the sugar is soluble. We say the sugar dissolves in the water to form a solution, which is clear.

Repeat the experiment, but this time add a teaspoonful of corn starch or flour to the warm water. Is corn starch or flour soluble in water?

Of course some substances that are soluble in water aren't soluble in other liquids, and some substances that aren't soluble in water are soluble in other liquids. You can see this for yourself. Add a pinch of sugar to a few milliliters of methanol in a small jar or a test tube. **Caution! methanol (wood alcohol) is poisonous and flammable.** Stir the mixture. Is sugar soluble in methanol?

Add a pinch of moth flakes to a few milliliters of methanol. Add a similar amount to a few milliliters of water. Stir both mixtures. Are moth flakes soluble in methanol? In water?

If a substance dissolves, or partially dissolves, in water, the next question to be tested is, How soluble is it? The *solubility* of a substance is defined as the number of grams that will dissolve in 100 g (or 1 g) of water at a particular temperature. You can determine the solubility of ordinary salt (sodium chloride) at room temperature by finding out how much of it dissolves in a known mass of water.

Pour about 20 mL of tap water into a small bottle or a large test tube. Add half a teaspoonful of kosher salt to the water, cover, and shake until all the salt dissolves. (Kosher salt is recommended because it has none of the impurities found in most table salt.) Continue adding the salt in half-teaspoonful amounts and shaking until no more salt will dissolve. When no more salt will dissolve, the solution is said to be saturated.

Use a balance to find the mass of a teacup or an evaporating dish. After recording the mass of the cup or dish, pour some of the saturated solution into the teacup or evaporating dish. Be sure that none of the solid salt at the bottom of the solution is poured off with the water. Reweigh the cup or dish. What is the mass of the solution (water and dissolved salt)?

Place the cup or dish in a warm place so that the water will evaporate, leaving the dissolved salt behind. This may take several days, depending on how warm the place is and how much solution you have. When all the water has evaporated and the salt is dry, reweigh the cup or dish. Weigh it again after several hours to be sure there is no further change in mass. If there is, continue to dry and reweigh until the mass remains constant. How much water evaporated? How much salt remains?

Since you now know the mass of the salt that dissolved and the mass of the water it was dissolved in, you can calculate the solubility of salt in water at room temperature. What is the solubility of salt (sodium chloride) in water according to your data?

If possible, borrow some sodium nitrate from your school and determine its solubility in the same way. Is sodium nitrate more or less soluble than sodium chloride?

It's possible to determine the solubility of various salts at different temperatures, but it's not easy to do without a laboratory where temperatures can be controlled. Figure 7 is a graph showing the solubility of several salts at different temperatures. Use the graph to compare the solubilities of sodium chloride and sodium nitrate at different temperatures. What do you notice?

Which salt in Figure 7 is least soluble at room temperature? Which salt shows the greatest increase in solubility with temperature? Do any of the salts show a decrease in solubility as the temperature increases?

Investigation 13: Other Solutions

MATERIALS NEEDED
- Water and rubbing alcohol
- Small jar or test tube
- Glass of cold water

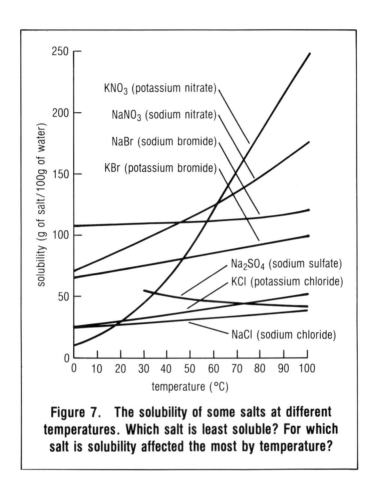

Figure 7. The solubility of some salts at different temperatures. Which salt is least soluble? For which salt is solubility affected the most by temperature?

Solids dissolved in liquids are not the only solutions. What happens if you mix two liquids such as water and alcohol in a small jar or test tube? Try it! Do they dissolve in one another?

From an earlier experiment you know what happens when you attempt to mix cooking oil and water. Are cooking oil and water soluble in one another?

It's obvious that gases dissolve in each other.

After all, air is a transparent mixture of nitrogen (78 percent), oxygen (21 percent), argon (1 percent), and small amounts of carbon dioxide, water vapor, neon, helium, and other gases.

If you've ever opened a bottle or a can of carbonated beverage, you know that gases dissolve in liquids. The carbon dioxide that dissolved in cola or ginger ale under high pressure is less soluble at atmospheric pressure. As a result, it bubbles out of the solution when you open the soda to the air. Unlike the solubility of most solids dissolved in liquids, the solubility of gases in liquids decreases as temperature rises. Leave a glass of cold water in a warm room. After an hour or two, look closely at the liquid. How can you explain the small bubbles you see in the liquid?

Puzzler 3: How Can You Dissolve a Fraction of a Drop?

How can you obtain a glass of water that contains just one-quarter of a drop of milk? How can you obtain a glass of water that contains just 1/100 teaspoonful of salt?

SINK

OR

FLOAT

In Chapter 2 you found by experiment that both alcohol and cooking oil are less dense than water. You also found that while alcohol and water dissolve (are miscible) in one another, cooking oil and water do not mix (are not miscible). Instead of mixing with water, cooking oil floats on it. The failure of oil and water to dissolve in one another explains the oil slicks you may have seen on puddles in a street. It also explains why oil spilled from large tankers floats on the sea and may be driven onshore by the wind. Will other substances with specific gravities less than 1.0 also float on water? Is it possible to form separate layers of substances even if they are miscible?

Investigation 14: Floaters and Sinkers

MATERIALS NEEDED
- Ruler • Block of wood • Laboratory balance • Stones or nails
- Water • Graduated cylinder

55

Use a ruler to find the dimensions of a wooden block. What is the volume of the block? Place the block on a laboratory balance and find its mass. What is the density of the wood? Do you think it will sink or float when placed in water? Try it! Were you right?

Find the density of some stones or steel nails. You can weigh them on a balance. To find the volume of irregularly shaped objects such as stones, place them in a known volume of water in a graduated cylinder. The volume of water they displace can be determined by observing the water level in the graduated cylinder after the objects are added. What is the volume of these objects?

According to the measurements, what is the density of the stones or nails? Do you think they will float or sink if placed on water? Try it! Were you right?

From the experiments you have done, how can you tell whether a substance will sink or float when dropped into water?

Puzzler 4: Can You Empty a Glass under Water?

A glass or plastic tumbler is submerged in a large pan of water and filled with water. How can you fill the glass with air without removing it from the water?

Puzzler 5: How Much of Sand Is Air?

How could you find the volume of some particles of sand? (Just the volume of the particles! Not the air that lies between the particles.) How can you find the volume of the air between the particles of sand?

Investigation 15: Floaters, Sinkers, and a Density Order

MATERIALS NEEDED

- Kosher salt, water, and container • Red and blue food coloring
- Small cylindrical glass or jar • Pipette, long eyedropper, or eyedropper with a soda straw attached • Small plastic vials • Freezer
- Eyedropper

Sometimes miscible liquids of different densities remain separated for quite some time if they are not stirred. Place a layer of a colored salt solution below some plain water. Prepare the salt solution by dissolving as much salt as you can in about 50 mL of water. Use kosher salt if possible; it has none of the impurities found in many table salts. Add a few drops of red food coloring to the solution so it can be readily identified.

Nearly fill a small cylindrical drinking or jelly glass with cold water. Then, using a pipette, a long eyedropper, or an eyedropper with a soda straw attached, place a layer of the red solution under the colorless water in the glass. See Figure 8.

What does this experiment tell you about the density of salt water as compared with plain water? Cover the glass and place it in a quiet place where it will not be disturbed. How long does the red salt solution take to spread evenly throughout the water?

Prepare a second glass of water with a layer of red salt solution in the same way and set it aside for a few hours. You will use these layered liquids after you prepare a piece of ice. Pour some water into a small plastic vial, such as a pill bottle. Add two or three

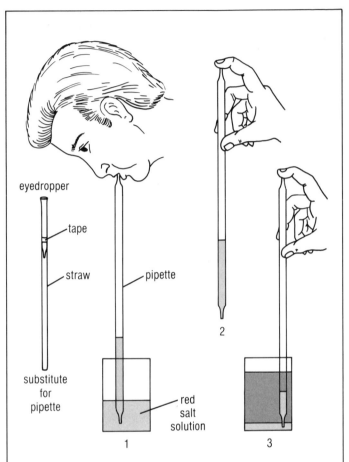

eyedropper

tape

straw

pipette

substitute for pipette

red salt solution

1

2

3

Figure 8. A pipette, or a substitute for a pipette, can be used to place a layer of red salt solution underneath some clear water. (1) Carefully draw some solution into the tube in strawlike fashion with your mouth. (2) Quickly cover the top of the pipette with your fingertip and carry the pipette to the clear water. (3) Put the lower end of the pipette on the bottom of the water. Lift your fingertip slightly so the salt solution can flow out of the pipette and under the water.

drops of blue food coloring to the water and place the container in a freezer. A few hours later, after the water has frozen, you will have a blue ice "cube." Remove the vial from the freezer, and run some tap water along the outside of the vial so that the blue ice will slide from its container.

Carefully place the ice on the surface of the second glass of liquid layers you set aside. What evidence do you have to show that ice is less dense than water?

Watch what happens to the blue ice as it melts in the water. Does the cold, blue melt water float or sink in the colorless warmer water? Does it float on or sink beneath the red salt solution? What does this tell you about the density of cold water as compared with cool or warm water? As compared with a salt solution?

As a further test, pour some cold tap water into a clear vial. Add a drop or two of food coloring to a second vial before you fill it with hot tap water. Remove some of the colored hot water with an eyedropper. Carefully place the end of the eyedropper in the cold water and *very gently* squeeze a little of the colored hot water into the center of the cold water. Does the colored hot water sink or rise in the cold water?

Repeat the experiment, but this time add food coloring to the cold water. If you gently squeeze a drop or two of the colored cold water into a vial of colorless hot water, do you think the cold water will sink or rise in the hot water? Try it! Were you right?

It's fun to arrange the liquids you've worked with in layers ordered according to their densities. You can do this very nicely in a clear plastic soda straw. You'll need more of the red salt solution you prepared earlier

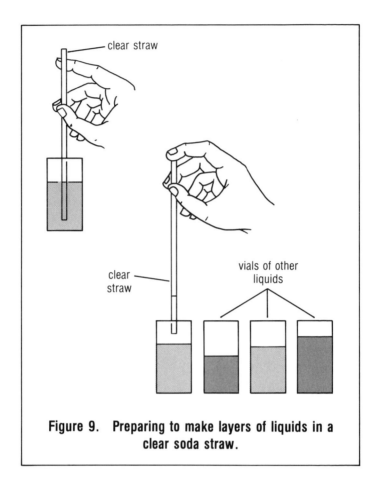

Figure 9. Preparing to make layers of liquids in a clear soda straw.

as well as some water colored with blue food coloring, cooking oil, and alcohol.

Put the empty straw into the blue water as shown in Figure 9. Then, as you've seen, if you place the tip of your index finger firmly on the top of the straw, you can lift the straw and the liquid will not run out. The liquid falls just a little in the straw, which increases the volume of the air trapped above the liquid. The increase in volume reduces the pressure of the air above the liquid so that the pressure of the air outside the straw is now greater than the pressure inside. Consequently, the liquid remains in the straw. The pressure of the air below the straw balances the pressure due to the weight of the liquid and the pressure of the air above it.

Lower the straw and blue water into the red salt solution until the level of the salt solution is *higher* than the water level in the straw. When you remove your fingertip from the top of the straw, the red solution will enter the bottom of the straw. Replace your fingertip and you can lift the straw with its two layers of liquid from the solution. Now, see whether you can make four layers of liquid in the straw using cooking oil and alcohol as well as the red and blue liquids. What happens if you try to place a less dense liquid below a more dense liquid?

Can you use other liquids, such as cranberry juice, apple juice, and cream, to make many layers of liquids in the straw? How can you tell the density order of the liquids?

TURNOVER

The experiments you have just done reveal what goes on every year in the lakes and ponds of regions where ice forms in the winter. During the autumn as the surface of a lake cools, the cool water sinks, forcing warmer water to the surface, where it too will cool. The solubility of oxygen in water, like that of all gases, increases as the temperature decreases. The increased concentration of oxygen in the water is carried downward to plants and animals on the lake's bottom. At the same time, the warmer upward-moving water carries the nutrient-rich sediment from the lake's bottom to organisms near the surface.

This circulation or turnover of water continues until the water reaches its maximum density at 4°C (see Figure 10). After the surface water temperature falls below 4°C, it tends to float on the denser 4-degree water below. When the temperature of the surface water reaches 0°C, it begins to freeze. Because water expands as it freezes, solid water (ice) is about 8 percent less dense than the water on which it floats.

Were it not for water's uncommon property of expanding as it freezes, ice would sink and lakes would freeze from bottom to top, killing most of the deep-dwelling organisms.

Investigation 16: A Model of Turnover

MATERIALS NEEDED
- Dark soil • Large glass or plastic tumbler
- Ice water and food coloring

You can demonstrate the effects of turnover quite easily. Put a small amount of soil in a tall clear plastic tumbler. Then add water to the tumbler until it is about three-quarters full. Allow the sediment in the dark mixture to settle for 24 hours. After most of the sediment has settled to the bottom, gently pour about 50 mL of colored ice water onto the surface of the water near one side of the tumbler. What happens as the cold water sinks to the bottom of the tumbler?

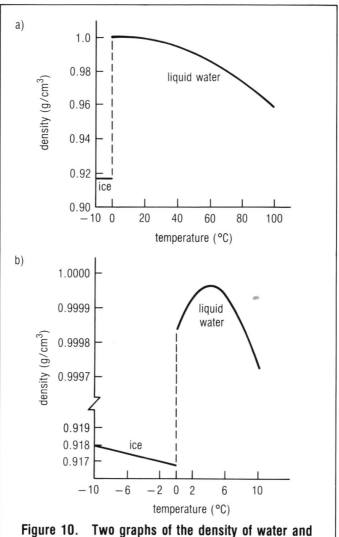

Figure 10. Two graphs of the density of water and ice versus temperature. (a) On a scale from −10 to 100 °C; (b) on a scale from −10 to 10 °C. At what temperature does ice have its maximum density? What happens to the density of ice as it cools below 0 °C?

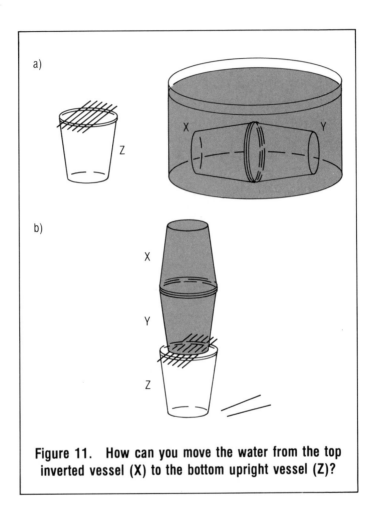

a)

X Y

Z

b)

X

Y

Z

Figure 11.   How can you move the water from the top inverted vessel (X) to the bottom upright vessel (Z)?

Puzzler 6: A Water Moving Puzzler

Obtain a few (six to ten) hollow cocktail stirrers. Place four or five of them on the top of an empty upright plastic tumbler (Z) as shown in Figure 11a. Submerge two more plastic tumblers (X and Y), identical to Z, in a large pan of water. To prevent spilling or leakage, the plastic tumblers *should have reasonably wide lips. (**If you work with an adult,** you can use glass tumblers.) Hold the mouths of the tumblers together, remove them from the water, and place them on top of the empty tumbler as shown in Figure 11b.*

Now, here's the puzzle! Without touching or moving the tumblers or the stirrers supporting the upper two water-filled tumblers, move the water from the uppermost inverted tumbler (X) to the bottom upright empty tumbler (Z). You may use an extra hollow stirrer but nothing else.

EUREKA!

There may be some truth to the story of Archimedes sitting in his bath contemplating a problem posed to him by his king, Hiero II. The king had asked Archimedes to find out whether a crown made for him by a goldsmith contained only gold as the king had requested. Archimedes used his surroundings—his bath water—in a very productive but accidental way to solve the problem he had wrestled with for some time. He suddenly realized that he could use a characteristic property of a substance—its density—to differentiate it from other substances.

Archimedes was probably not the first person to observe, as you probably have, that your body feels lighter when it displaces water while sinking into a bathtub of water. But it was Archimedes who first understood what underlies this feeling and thereby put us on the proper path to explaining why some things sink and others float.

Investigation 17: Archimedes' Principle

MATERIALS NEEDED

- Thread or string • Large piece of metal—lead sinker, metal cylinder or cube, stack of coins tied together, and so on. • Ruler or large graduated cylinder • Overflow can and small graduated cylinder • Soapy water and container • Paper towels • Spring balance or laboratory balance • Ring stand and ring or steady hand • Water and alcohol or other liquid such as witch hazel or mineral oil

When Archimedes leaped from his bath, he may or may not have run through the streets shouting, "Eureka! Eureka!" But it's quite certain that he turned to his laboratory to test his inspiration. And you can do the same.

From a thread or string, suspend a fairly large piece of metal such as a lead sinker, a metal cylinder or cube, a stack of coins tied together, or something similar. Find the volume of the object by measuring its dimensions or by submerging it in a partially filled graduated cylinder to see how much water it displaces. If it is too large to fit into a graduated cylinder, use an overflow can filled with soapy water as shown in Figure 12a (2). The water displaced flows out of the can and can be collected in a graduated cylinder. (You'll learn in Chapter 4 why soapy water should be used.)

After drying the object, weigh it in air and then in water (Figure 12b). You can weigh the object with a spring balance or a laboratory balance if you keep the container in which the object is submerged off the balance pan.

How does the object's loss of weight in water compare with the weight of the water it displaces?

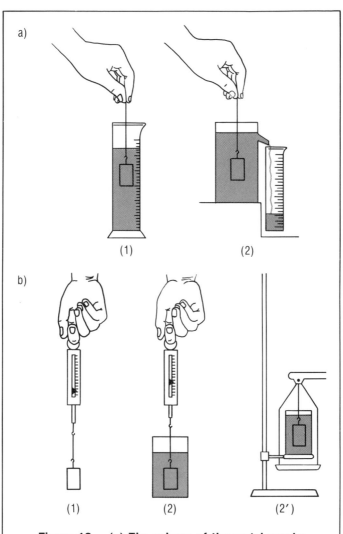

Figure 12. (a) The volume of the metal can be determined by measuring dimensions or by submerging the object in a partially filled graduated cylinder (1), or by using an overflow can (2). (b) The object's weight can be measured in air (1) and while submerged in water (2) or (2′).

Since the density of water is 1g/cm^3, you can easily determine the weight of the water displaced.

Try the experiment with several different objects including at least one that floats. How does the object's loss of weight in water compare with the weight of the water displaced? What happens if you submerge or float the object in a different liquid such as alcohol? How does the loss of weight when it is submerged or floating in the liquid compare with the weight of the liquid displaced?

Investigation 18: Boats, Draft, and Cargo

MATERIALS NEEDED
- Tuna fish can • Pennies, other coins, or water and graduated cylinder
- Balance and ruler • Wood and clay

From what you have learned, you can make some rather surprising predictions about boats and the cargo they can carry. For your "boat," you can use an empty tuna fish can. Pennies, other identical coins, or measured volumes of water can serve as cargo.

Begin by weighing the boat and ten pieces of cargo. (If you use water as the cargo, the volume of the water, in milliliters or cubic centimeters, will give you the weight of the cargo in grams.) Then measure the diameter and height of your tuna-can boat.

Using Archimedes' principle, what volume of water will the can displace when placed on water? From the information you have gathered, predict the depth to which the boat will sink in water. (This is referred to as the boat's draft.) Try it! Were you close?

Next, predict the maximum weight of the cargo

Why does a large ship, which is made of steel, float in water?

your boat can hold without sinking. Don't forget that the boat has weight, too. Then slowly and gently add the cargo to the boat, being careful to keep it spread evenly so the boat does not tip. What is the maximum weight of cargo that the boat will hold? How closely does it agree with the value you predicted?

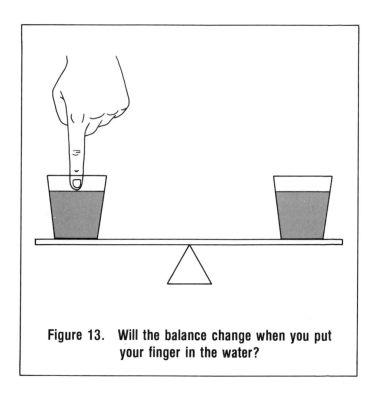

Figure 13. Will the balance change when you put your finger in the water?

Will this boat sink if you submerge it in water? Why? Will a wooden boat sink if submerged in water?

Place a lump of clay in a pan of water. Does the clay sink? What does this tell you about the density of clay? What can you do to make the clay float on water?

Puzzler 7: An Archimedes' Water and Balance Puzzler

Two small containers half-filled with water are balanced at opposite ends of a small seesaw as shown in Figure 13. What will happen if you stick the end of your finger in one of the containers?

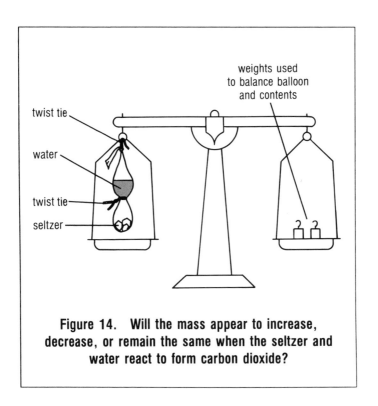

Figure 14. Will the mass appear to increase, decrease, or remain the same when the seltzer and water react to form carbon dioxide?

Puzzler 8: An Archimedes' Balloon, Air, and Gas Puzzler

Suppose you have an inflatable bag or balloon suspended from one side of a balance beam as shown in Figure 14. At the bottom of the bag are the broken pieces of a seltzer tablet or powdered seltzer. Above the seltzer is some water, which can be released onto the seltzer by removing the twist tie. (To be sure the mass doesn't change, the twist tie that is removed should remain on the balance.) As you may know, water reacts with seltzer to produce carbon dioxide gas, which is about 1.5 times as dense as air. As this gas is produced, the bag or balloon expands. Will the mass of the bag and contents appear to increase, decrease, or remain the same?

WATER, FORCES, PRESSURE, BOATS, AND BALLOONS

Archimedes' principle, which you discovered in Investigation 17, states that an object is buoyed upward by a force equal to the weight of the fluid it displaces. Usually, but not always, the fluid is water. It may be any liquid or a gas. After all, hot air balloons are buoyed upward by the cold air that surrounds them. But you may wonder, as others did, why there is a buoyant force on objects submerged in a fluid.

Have you ever tried to push a beach ball under the water? If you have, you know that it takes a large force to submerge the ball. Furthermore, when you release the ball, the water exerts an upward force that propels the ball high into the air. The force on the ball arises because of a pressure that increases with depth in water.

FORCE, MASS, AND WEIGHT • More than 300 years ago Sir Isaac Newton showed the world that if an object with a mass, m, is near the earth's surface, the force of gravity on that object is given by

$$F = mg,$$

where g is a constant that depends on the mass and radius of the planet. In the case of Earth, g has a value of 9.8 N/kg. Thus, a 1 kilogram mass has a weight of 9.8 newtons:

$$F = 1.0 \text{ kg} \times 9.8 \text{ N/kg} = 9.8 \text{ N}.$$

On the moon, where g has a value of 1.7 N/kg, the same 1 kilogram mass would weigh 1.7 N. The moon's gravity does not pull as hard on the object as the earth's does.

PRESSURE • The pressure exerted by a gas, liquid, or solid is defined as the force per unit area. This can be expressed mathematically as

$$P = \frac{F}{A},$$

where P is the pressure, F the force, and A the area on which the force acts.

If a man weighing 1000 N has shoes with a total area of 0.025 m^2 (250 cm^2) in contact with the floor, he will exert a pressure of

$$\frac{1000 \text{ N}}{0.025} = 40,000 \text{ N/m}^2 \quad \text{or} \quad \frac{1000 \text{ N}}{250 \text{ cm}^2} = 4 \text{ N/cm}^2 \text{ on the floor.}$$

Suppose a woman weighing 500 N is wearing high heels and the total shoe area in contact with the floor under her feet is 0.010 m^2 (100 cm^2). What pressure will she exert on the floor?

Investigation 19: Pressure and Direction

MATERIALS NEEDED
- Rubber dam or plastic wrap • Small funnel or thistle tube • Rubber band • Rubber tubing • Glass tubing • Water and food coloring
- Large clear container, e.g., a fish tank

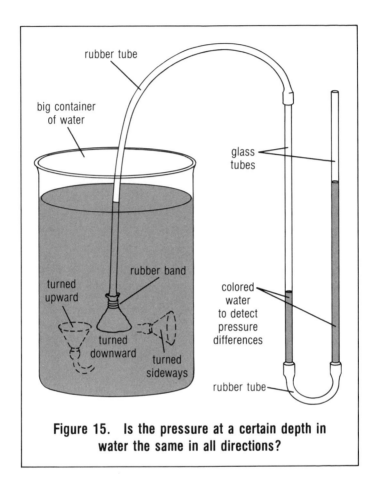

Figure 15. Is the pressure at a certain depth in water the same in all directions?

In the last paragraph you read that the pressure of the air acts upward as well as downward. To see whether pressure really is exerted equally in all directions, you can build a simple pressure measuring device like the one shown in Figure 15. A sheet of rubber dam or plastic wrap is pulled tightly over a small funnel or thistle tube and fastened securely with a rubber band. One end of a rubber tube is connected to the stem of the funnel or thistle tube; the other end is connected to a U-shaped tube partially filled with colored water as shown. When the funnel or tube is lowered into a deep container of water, the liquid in the U-tube is forced into the right-hand side, indicating that the pressure exerted by the liquid increases with depth. If you've ever dived into water, this probably doesn't surprise you. But now turn the covered end of the tube so that it faces sideways or even upward. If you keep the center of the surface of the rubber or plastic wrap covering the mouth of the funnel or tube at the same depth in the water regardless of its orientation, what do you find is true of the pressure?

Investigation 20: Pressure and Depth

MATERIALS NEEDED
- Large metal can • Hammer and nail • Masking tape • Water
- Aneroid barometer

Another way to see how pressure increases with depth is to take a large can and use a hammer and nail to punch holes in its side at various heights from bottom to top. Cover the holes with masking tape. Place the can near a sink and fill it with water. The pressure of the water will exert a force across the area of each hole. The greater the pressure, the greater the force.

Now quickly remove the tape from the holes. How can you tell that the pressure increases with the depth of the water?

Does the same hold true for a gas? Suppose you go up into the atmosphere. Does the pressure of the air decrease? You can find out by reading an aneroid barometer (the kind you find on walls in homes) at the bottom and top of a tall building or a high hill. How does the air pressure at the top of the building or hill compare with the pressure at the bottom?

Take an aneroid barometer with you on an automobile trip through some hilly country. Can you predict when the pressure will increase? When it will decrease?

PRESSURE AND DEPTH

You've seen that the pressure increases as the depth below the surface of water increases. In fact, careful measurements show that the pressure due to water is proportional to depth: that is, doubling the depth doubles the water pressure. Of course, there is also air pressure near the earth's surface, which adds to the pressure exerted by the water.

To see why pressure is proportional to depth, and why Archimedes' principle is true, consider the diagram in Figure 16. A block B is at rest with its top at the level of the liquid in which it lies. Now consider the pressure due to the liquid on the bottom of the block. The dotted lines show a column of liquid with a height h and a square base $x \times x$. The height of the liquid column, h, is the same as the height of the block, which has a base $L \times L$. The volume of the column of liquid is x^2h, and its mass, m, is equal to its density, d, times its volume, x^2h. Therefore, the mass of the liquid is equal to dx^2h, and the weight of the liquid, mg, is dx^2hg.

Consider the small imaginary square, $x \times x$, at

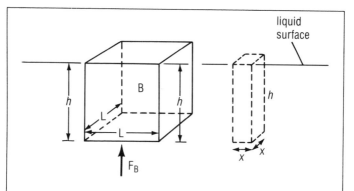

liquid
surface

Figure 16. An explanation of how pressure is related to depth and Archimedes' Principle. In the diagram, density, d, equals mass, m, per unit volume, V, or $d = \dfrac{m}{V}$. The weight, W, of a liquid is its mass $\times$ g. For the small column of liquid shown in dotted lines, $W = mg = (dx^2h)g$. The pressure, P, at the base of this column is given by $P = \dfrac{F}{A} = \dfrac{dx^2hg}{x^2} = dhg$. The buoyant force, F_B, on the block, B, is given by $F_B = P \times A = dhg \times L^2$, but L^2h is the volume of the water displaced; therefore, the weight of the water displaced is given by $W = dL^2hg$, which is equal to the buoyant force, F_B.

the base of the column of liquid in Figure 16. The pressure (the force divided by the area) produced by the weight of the liquid above the square is the weight of the column of water divided by the area of the square. The pressure, therefore, is

$$\frac{dx^2hg}{x^2} = dhg.$$

This tells us that the pressure at a depth h in a liquid is equal to the density of the liquid, d, times the depth, h, times g. It also tells us that for any given liquid the pressure is proportional to the depth of the liquid because the density and g are constant near the earth's surface.

Now consider the block, B, which has a volume L^2h. The force on the top of the block is air pressure times the area of the block's top surface. (Since $P = F/A$, $F = P \times A$.) The force due to air pressure will also act on the bottom of the block, but there will be an additional force on the bottom of the block because it is beneath the water. You've seen that the water pressure at the depth of the block's bottom will be dhg. The upward or buoyant force, F_B, due to this water pressure is the pressure times the area of the block's base or $dhg \times L^2$.

The volume of water displaced by the block is L^2h, and the weight of this water is dL^2hg, which is the same as the buoyant force, F_B. Thus, the buoyant force is equal to the weight of the liquid displaced.

Puzzler 9: Keeping Water in an Upside-Down Tube

Fill a large medicine vial or a test tube brimful with water. Then add some water to a shallow dish beside the vial. Place a square piece of paper towel about 2 inches on a side beside the vial. How can you invert the water-filled vial into the water without spilling the water and without covering the vial with your hand or fingers?

Puzzler 10: Sipping Soda with a Holey Straw

Use a small nail to punch a hole about 2 inches from one end of a soda straw. Place the other end in a glass of water. Can you use the straw to drink water from the glass?

Puzzler 11: Can You Drink Water from a Straw in a Sealed Bottle?

Place a soda straw in a bottle of soda. Seal the open space between the straw and the neck of the bottle with clay. Why can't you drink from the bottle through the straw?

WATER IS STICKIER
THAN
YOU THINK

You probably don't think of water as a sticky substance. In fact, you often use soap and water to wash your sticky hands. That's because you probably think of a sticky substance as one that sticks to your skin. But suppose you think about internal stickiness—the tendency of a substance to hold itself together. The attraction of the molecules within a substance for one another is called cohesion, and cohesive forces hold like molecules together. Adhesive forces—the forces we normally associate with stickiness—are due to the forces of attraction between *different* substances. There are strong adhesive properties between glue and paper or athletic tape and skin. The element mercury has strong cohesive forces. It holds together very well.

SURFACE TENSION

Have you ever noticed insects standing or walking on the surface of the water in a pond? If you look closely,

Liquid mercury holds together very well. It has strong cohesive forces between its molecules.

you'll see dimples where the water is slightly depressed beneath their feet. Water's surface behaves as if it had a skin, as if it were under tension like a stretched rubber membrane. The next investigation will help you to see water's "skin."

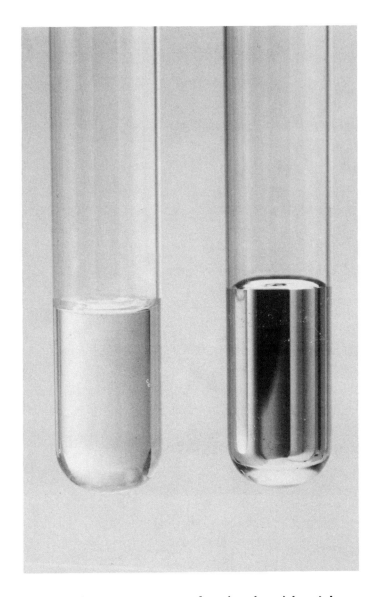

Water forms a concave surface (meniscus) in a tube because of the strong adhesive forces between water and glass (left). On the other hand, mercury's internal cohesive forces are stronger than the adhesive forces between the metal and glass (right).

Investigation 21: Water's "Skin"

MATERIALS NEEDED
- Glass or plastic container • Water • Dining fork • Paper clip
- Soap solution • Rubbing alcohol • Medicine cup or pill vial
- Eyedroppers • Waxed paper, aluminum foil, plastic wrap, newspaper, glass • Cooking oil

The following activities reveal that the surface of water behaves as if it had a skin. They will also show you how that property can be changed, and how it is less evident in other substances. In all the activities, be sure the container is clean and has been thoroughly rinsed with water. The presence of soap or dirt will change water's "skin."

WATER'S SUPPORTIVE SKIN • Pour some water into a clean glass or plastic container. When the surface of the water has stopped moving, use a clean table fork to place a paper clip gently on the water's surface. Notice how the water surface is depressed where the paper clip rests. What happens when you add a drop of a soap solution to the water?

Do you think you can "float" a paper clip on soapy water? On rubbing alcohol? Try them! Were your predictions correct?

WHAT IS BRIMFUL? • Add water to a medicine cup or a pill vial until it is level with the top of the container. Next, use a clean, well-rinsed eyedropper to add drops of water to the container. Can you make the water heap up above the top of the container? How many drops of water can you add to the brimful container before water finally runs down the sides?

**Water's "skin" can support a paper clip
and a razor blade. Observe how the "skin" is
stretched where the object pushes on it.**

Repeat the experiment, but this time before you add the maximum number of drops that can be heaped above the top, use a different eyedropper to add a drop of a soap solution. Are the results the same?

How many drops of soapy water can be heaped above the top of a brimful container of soapy water? Use a third eyedropper to find out how many drops of rubbing alcohol can be heaped above a brimful vial of alcohol.

DROPS AND SURFACES • From what you have seen in the previous investigations, see whether you can predict how drops of water, soapy water, and alcohol compare if placed on a sheet of waxed paper. After you've made your predictions, use the three separate eyedroppers you've used with the three liquids to place drops of water, soapy water, and alcohol on the waxed paper. Were your predictions right? Which drop seems to hold together best? Which drop seems to hold together least well?

Using the same eyedroppers as before, place a drop of water on the waxed paper. Then place a second drop very close to the first one. What happens when they meet? What evidence do you have to indicate that water is cohesive? Try the same experiment with two drops of soapy water. With two drops of alcohol. How do their cohesive properties compare with those of water?

Use a fourth eyedropper to add a drop of cooking oil to the waxed paper. How does it compare with the other drops you've tested?

Does the surface on which the drops are placed affect their shape? To find out, use the "water eyedropper" to place drops of water on sheets of aluminum foil, plastic wrap, newspaper, and glass as well as waxed paper. Why do you think the shape of a drop of water is affected by the kind of surface it is on?

Repeat the experiment using the appropriate eyedroppers for soapy water, alcohol, and cooking oil. Is the drop shape of these liquids affected by the surface they are on? How can you explain the differences you have observed?

- Using the same eyedropper as before, which of the liquids do you think will form the largest drops? Design an experiment to find out whether you are right.
- Having seen the shape of water drops, design your own water lens and use it as a magnifying glass. Can you also design a water-drop-lens microscope?

Puzzler 12: The Spoon and Dime Puzzler

Submerge two plastic tumblers in a large pan of water as you did in Puzzler 6 in Chapter 3. Place the mouths of the tumblers together, remove them from the water, and place them in a pan on top of a counter. Place a dime and a spoon beside the water-filled vessels, one of them inverted on the other. Using only the spoon, and without touching the tumblers with your hands, how can get the dime onto the bottom of the lower vessel?

SURFACE TENSION: AN EXPLANATION AND A DEFINITION

As you've seen, the cohesive forces between water molecules are stronger than those between the molecules of at least some other liquids. These cohesive forces can explain the "skinlike" properties of water's surface. Water molecules beneath the surface are pulled equally in all directions by the molecules that surround them as shown in Figure 17a. For molecules on or near the surface, there are many more molecules below than above them. Consequently, these surface or near-surface molecules "feel" a net force downward that draws them closer to their neighbors. As a result, these mole-

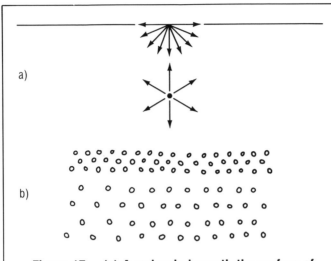

Figure 17. (a) A molecule beneath the surface of water is attracted equally in all directions by the molecules that surround it. A molecule on or near the surface has many more molecules attracting it from below than from above. Consequently, the net force on such a molecule is downward. (b) The result of these attractive forces is to increase the concentration of molecules near the surface. The strong attractive forces between molecules near the surface will resist any attempt to pull them apart.

cules are pulled tightly together, forming a boundary surface that is skinlike. Any attempt to stretch this surface will be resisted by the strong attractive forces between the molecules at the surface and those directly beneath them. See Figure 17*b*.

As a result of these cohesive forces, any line of molecules on the surface of the liquid is pulled by other molecules on both sides of the line. For example,

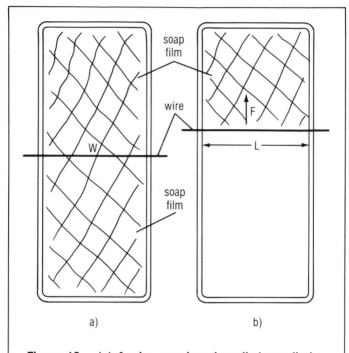

Figure 18. (a) A wire on a loop is pulled equally in both directions by the surfaces of a liquid film covering the loop. (b) When the film on one side of the wire is broken, the wire is pulled by the surface on the side where the film is still intact.

suppose a soap film covers the wire loop shown in Figure 18*a*. A wire, W, across the loop "feels" a force pulling it equally in both directions. If the film on one side is broken by piercing it with a pin, the wire will be pulled toward the side where the film remains. The surface tension of the film, *S*, is defined as the ratio of the force exerted by the surface to the length along which the force acts. In Figure 18*b*, the force is shown as F and the length of the wire on which it acts is L. Therefore, the surface tension is given by

$$S = \frac{F}{2\,L}.$$

The 2 in the denominator arises from the fact that the film has two surfaces (top and bottom), each of which acts along the length, L, of the wire.

Investigation 22: Measuring Surface Tension

MATERIALS NEEDED

• Light cotton thread • Wire • Soap solution such as a child's bubble-making solution • T-pins and common pins • Plastic soda straw • Scissors • Paper clips, large and small • Paper punch • Cardboard tube • Pliers and small nail • Candle and matches • Shallow container • Clay • Water and dilute soap solution (a few drops of liquid soap in cup of water) • Rubbing alcohol • Cardboard sheets (if necessary) • Eyedroppers and graduated cylinder • Paper towel

To see that a surface does indeed exert a force, you can tie a piece of light cotton thread on a wire loop as shown in Figure 19a. Dip the loop into a solution of soapy water so that a soap film covers the entire area inside the loop. Now use a pin or your fingertip to break the film on one side of the thread. What happens when the film breaks? What evidence do you have that the film's surfaces are under tension? That the forces were equal on both sides of the thread before the film broke?

Repeat the experiment, but this time make a loop in the thread as shown in Figure 19b, and break the

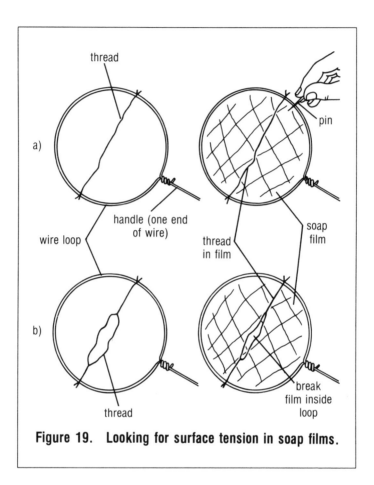

Figure 19. Looking for surface tension in soap films.

film inside the loop of thread. If you use a pin to break the film, it may be difficult to do. If it is, use the pin to widen the loop until you can touch it with your fingertip. What happens to the loop when the film within it is broken? How can you explain what happens?

To make a quantitative measurement of surface tension you will need a device to measure forces. You can do this by building a sensitive balance that can measure the small forces involved in surface tension. Using a plastic soda straw, pins, paper clips, thread, a medicine cup, and the cardboard tube from a roll of toilet paper, you can build a balance like the one shown in Figure 20.

Use scissors to cut a slot 1 cm long by 0.5 cm wide at each end of the straw. These slots will be on the bottom side of the soda-straw balance beam. Common pins should then be inserted 0.5 cm in from each end of the beam. Insert these pins above the slots, but be sure they lie *below* the long central axis of the straw. A paper clip will be hung from each pin so that balance pans and measuring devices can be attached to the balance beam.

It is important that the T-pin on which the soda straw balance beam will rotate go through the straw at a point midway between its ends. Be certain, however, that the pin is inserted *above* the midpoint of the straw. (Should the pin be inserted below the midpoint, the balance will be unstable.) Use scissors to cut slots on each side at the top of the cardboard tube so that the balance beam can swing up and down within the tube. Use a paper punch to make two holes on opposite sides near the top of the cardboard tube. These holes will support the T-pin on which the beam swings. **Have an adult help you** by using pliers to hold the end of another T-pin in a candle flame. The hot pin can be pushed through the plastic medicine cup to make two holes on opposite sides. Run a piece of thread through the holes and tie the ends so that the cup can be attached to a paper clip at

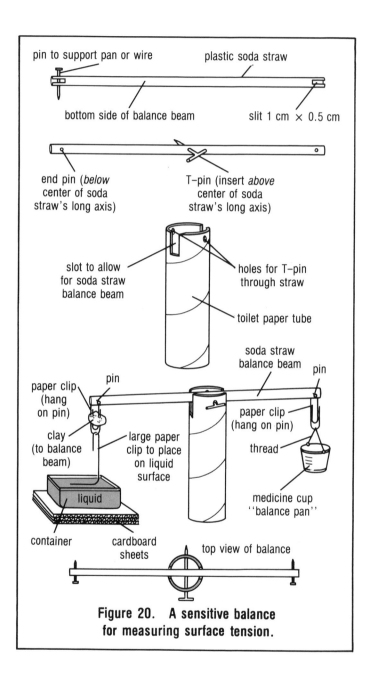

Figure 20. A sensitive balance for measuring surface tension.

one end of the beam. The cup will serve as a balance pan.

At the other end of the beam hang a large paper clip, which should be opened so that the long side of the clip can be placed on the surface of a liquid (see Figure 20). If the balance beam is not level, add a small piece of clay to the paper clip on one side of the beam until balance is achieved.

To measure the surface tension of water, add cold water to the shallow container. Place the container on cardboard sheets if necessary so that the long horizontal wire formed by the large bent paper clip touches the water's surface. With a clean eyedropper, gently add drops of water, one at a time, to the medicine cup balance pan attached to the other end of the beam. How many drops are required to overcome the force due to surface tension that holds the wire to the water's surface? Repeat the experiment several times to be sure your results are consistent.

Dry the medicine cup with a paper towel and repeat the experiment after replacing the water in the shallow container with a dilute soap solution. On the basis of earlier experiments, do you think fewer or more drops of water will have to be added to the balance pan to pull the wire from the soap solution? Try it! Were you right? How does the surface tension of soapy water compare with that of water?

Dry the medicine cup again, and rinse and dry the wire. Then repeat the experiment to find out how the surface tension of alcohol compares with that of water and soapy water. What do you find? Are your results

TABLE 3: The Surface Tension of a Number of Liquids as Measured by Experiment.

Liquid	Temperature (°C)	Surface Tension (dyn/cm)
Acetone	20	23.7
Grain alcohol	20	22.3
Glycerin	20	63.1
Mercury	20	470
Olive oil	20	32.0
Soapy water	20	25.0
Water	0	75.6
Water	20	72.7
Water	50	67.9
Water	60	66.2
Water	100	58.9
Oxygen	− 193	15.7
Neon	− 247	5.2
Helium	− 269	0.11

what you'd expect on the basis of experiments you've done before?

- Try the same experiments using the long edge of a glass microscope slide in place of the wire. How do the results compare?

COMPARING RESULTS

Table 3 contains information about the comparative surface tension of various liquids as measured in units of dynes/centimeter (dyn/cm) at 20°C. According to the table, water has a greater surface tension than either alcohol or soapy water. Do your results agree with those in the table?

You can also compare your numerical results with those in the table. Since the density of water is 1 g/mL, you can find the mass of one drop of water, which you used as your unit of mass. With the same eyedropper you used to add water to the balance pan and a graduated cylinder, find out how many drops are in 10 mL (10 g) of water. How can you use that information to find the mass of one drop?

What was the length of the wire that rested on the water in your experiment? The force due to gravity on a gram of water is about 1000 dynes. Use the information you've collected to convert your measurements to dynes per centimeter (dyn/cm). For example, suppose you had to add 12 drops of water to pull the wire off the surface of water. Suppose too that you found that there are 20 drops in a milliliter of water. Each drop then is 0.05 g ($\frac{1}{20}$ g), and, therefore, the mass of 12 drops is 0.60 g. The force of gravity acting on such a mass, which was the force needed to pull the water apart, would be about 600 dynes. If the length of the wire you placed on the water was 4.0 cm, then your calculation of the surface tension would be

$$S = \frac{F}{2\,L} = \frac{600 \text{ dyn}}{2 \times 4.0 \text{ cm}} = 75 \text{ dyn/cm.}$$

From the information given in the table, what happens to surface tension as the water temperature increases? As the water temperature decreases? See whether you can confirm these temperature effects by doing experiments of your own. Why do you think surface tension might change as it does with temperature? Do you think the surface tension of other liquids would change in the same way with temperature? What makes you think so?

Investigation 23: Stretching an Area of Water's Surface

MATERIALS NEEDED

- Flat pieces of plastic • Balance from last investigation • Scissors
- Metric ruler • Pliers • Common pins and thread • Shallow dish
- Cardboard • Eyedroppers • Hardware cloth and/or berry baskets
- Water, soap solution, rubbing alcohol

In the last investigation you measured the force along a line on a liquid's surface. Suppose you place the entire area of a square plate on the surface of some water. If the square has the same length as the wire you used before, do you think the force required to pull the area of liquid apart will be more or less than the force needed to pull the length of liquid apart? Do you think the force will change if the area of the plate is changed? If the shape of the plate is changed (with no change in area)? If different liquids are used?

In this investigation you'll have an opportunity to carry out some experiments that will allow you to check up on the predictions you made in answering these questions. The squares that you will need can be cut from flat pieces of plastic such as the tops of coffee cans or margarine tubs.

Using scissors, cut a square that is 4 cm on a side from a piece of plastic. **Ask an adult to help you** use pliers to push a common pin through the center of each square. Use the same pliers to bend the end of the pin.

Be sure the plastic adheres to water. You can check its adhesive properties by hanging a square from a piece of thread. Lower the plastic onto the surface of some water. Then gently lift it off the surface. Look at the bottom of the square. If there is water on its surface, it must have been the water that pulled apart. If there is no water, the adhesion between plate and water was less than the cohesion between the water molecules; the plate simply separated from the water. If the latter is the case, look for another kind of plastic that adheres more strongly to water.

Once you've found a plastic that adheres strongly to water, prepare additional squares that are 2, 3, 5, and 6 cm on a side. **Under adult supervision,** add pins so that the squares can be hung from the balance beam as shown in Figure 21.

After hanging a plastic plate from one end of the balance beam, adjust the balance until the beam is level. You can do this by adding a little clay to the paper clip at the end of one side of the beam as you did before. Now place a shallow dish of water under the plate. If necessary, use cardboard sheets to raise the dish until the water touches the plate. To see how much force is required to pull the plate off the water, you can again use an eyedropper to add drops of water to the pan suspended from the opposite end of the balance beam. Watch the plate closely as you add water drops to the pan. Can you see that the water adhering to the plate is being lifted by the force applied through

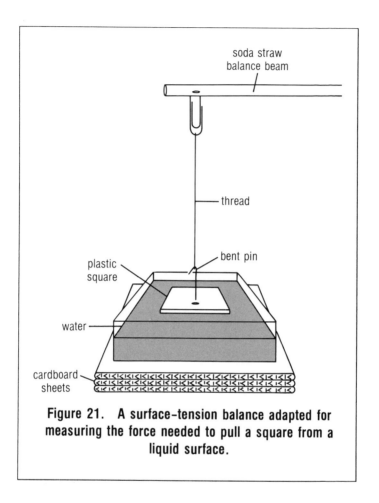

Figure 21. A surface-tension balance adapted for measuring the force needed to pull a square from a liquid surface.

the balance? In addition to stretching the water's surface, the force applied to the balance is lifting a small volume of water. Estimate the volume of water that is lifted before the water breaks apart.

Compare the forces, in units of water drops, required to pull each of the different size squares off the surface of the water. Plot a graph of the force required to pull the plate off the water versus the area of the plate. How is the force related to the area of the square?

- Prepare other plates with different shapes—circle, rectangle, triangle, and other polygons—that have the same area (16 cm^2) as the 4 cm × 4 cm square plate. Does the shape make a difference in the force required to pull the plate apart? How can you explain your results?
- Try squares made from window screen or berry baskets that have a gridlike structure. Is the force required to pull water apart using these squares more, less, or the same as that with plastic plates of the same area?
- Design an experiment that will enable you to measure the maximum volume of water lifted by each of the plates you have used.
- Estimate the force, in drops of water, that will be required to pull each of the plates you've tested from alcohol and from a soap solution. Then test your estimates by experiment. How good were your estimates? Were any of them way off? If so, can you now in retrospect explain why your estimate was in error?

Investigation 24: Beading Streams of Water

MATERIALS NEEDED
- T-pin or hat pin • Foam plastic cups • Nails of increasing size: 3d, 6d, . . . , 16d • Sharp knife or razor blade • Sink, water, and pan (optional) • Ruler

Turn a faucet very slightly so that only a very thin stream of water emerges. Notice how the stream pulls together to form drops. You might say that the continu-

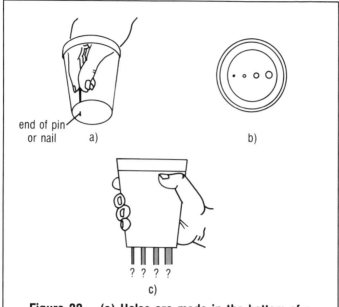

end of pin or nail a) b)

c)

Figure 22. (a) Holes are made in the bottom of a foam plastic cup. The pin or nail is pushed through the cup from the inside to the outside. (b) Several holes of increasing diameter are made across the bottom of the cup. (c) The cup is filled with water and held motionless above a sink. Which stream beads first? Which stream falls farthest before beading?

ous stream becomes beaded. Why do you think the water pulls together into drops? Which do you think will form drops first, a thin or a thick stream of water?

You can answer the second question by doing an experiment. Use a T-pin or a hat pin to make a hole in the bottom of a plastic foam cup. Make the hole near one side of the cup, as shown in Figure 22, by pushing the pin through the cup from the inside to the outside.

Make three or four more holes in the same way using nails of increasing size (none larger than 16d). Be sure the holes are at least 0.75 cm apart. Then **ask an adult to help you** trim away any loose material from around the holes on the outside of the cup with a sharp knife or razor blade.

Take the cup to a sink. Fill it with water and hold it motionless above the sink. Look at the different size streams as they emerge from the bottom of the cup. Which stream beads first? Is it the one you predicted would bead first? What happens to the length of the continuous unbeaded stream as the diameter of the stream increases?

If you have difficulty seeing the place where beading first occurs in a stream, you can use a sound method to find the beading point. To do this, punch a *single* hole in the bottom of a cup. Fill the cup with water and hold it over a pan partially filled with water. Start with the cup high above the pan. You'll hear the drops spatter as they hit the water in the pan. Now lower the cup. What happens to the sound when you reach a point where the stream entering the water in the pan is unbeaded or continuous? How can you use this change in sound to identify the beading point?

Repeat the experiment several times. Each time use a cup that has a hole with a different diameter. How does the beading point change as the diameter of the stream increases?

- Measure the lengths of the unbeaded streams, that is, the distance from the bottom of the cup to the beading point for each stream. Also measure the diameters of the holes from which the streams emerge. Plot a graph of the length of the unbeaded stream versus the diameter of the hole through which the stream flows. Can you find any relationship between these two variables?

- Use a small nail to punch three holes within a few millimeters of one another in the bottom of a plastic foam cup. Fill the cup with water and let the three streams flow through the holes. Use your finger and thumb to "squeeze" the streams together. What happens when the streams touch one another? Can you explain why the streams fuse together?

Investigation 25: Beading Points and Different Liquids

MATERIALS NEEDED
- Foam plastic cups • Average size nail, e.g., 6d
- Sharp knife or razor blade • Sink, water, and pan • Ruler
- Soap solution • Alcohol

From experiments that you have done earlier, try to predict how the beading points of different liquids will compare. For instance, suppose you have a cup of water and a cup of soapy water. The bottoms of both cups have holes of exactly the same size. Which liquid will have the longer unbeaded column; that is, for which liquid will the beading point be farther from the bottom of the cup?

To test your prediction, use a cup with a medium size hole in the bottom. A hole made with a 6d nail is good. Fill the cup with water and find the length of the unbeaded column using the sound method described in the previous experiment. Once you have found the beading point, use a ruler to measure the distance from the bottom of the cup to the surface of the water in the pan. How long was the unbeaded or continuous stream?

Repeat the experiment using soapy water in the cup. How long is the unbeaded stream this time? Was your prediction correct?

Estimate the length of an unbeaded stream of alcohol emerging through the same opening. Then check your estimate. How close was your estimate to the experimental value you found?

Investigation 26: A Tug-of-War

MATERIALS NEEDED
- Light thread and scissors • Shallow container with water
- Eyedropper • Soapy water • Alcohol

You've seen what happens when a liquid surface pulls on a thread suspended in a film of the liquid (Investigation 22), but what will happen if two different liquid surfaces pull the thread in opposite directions? Which liquid will win the tug-of-war? You can probably predict the outcome on the basis of experiments you have done before.

Place a loop of light thread on the surface of some water in a shallow container. As you can see, the thread assumes no particular shape because it is pulled equally on all sides by the water surface. What do you think will happen if you use an eyedropper to place a drop of soapy water *inside* the loop? Try it! Were you able to predict the outcome?

Try the same experiment using alcohol in place of soapy water. Can you predict the outcome of this experiment?

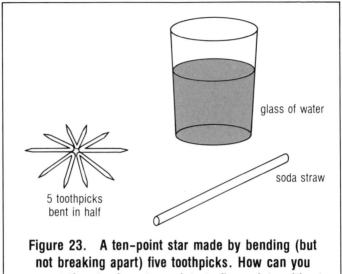

Figure 23. A ten-point star made by bending (but not breaking apart) five toothpicks. How can you convert the star from ten points to five points without touching the toothpicks?

Puzzler 13: A Starry Puzzler

Bend five toothpicks in half. Arrange them in the form of a ten-pointed star near a glass of water and a straw as shown in Figure 23. How can you or anyone else change the ten-pointed star to a five-pointed star without touching the toothpicks?

Puzzler 14: A Brush In and Out of Water

Examine a dry camel's-hair brush. Notice how the hairs remain apart. Now wet the brush by dipping it in water. When you hold the wet brush in air, the hairs cling together. Is this because they are wet? Apparently not, because if you dip the brush in a clear glass of water you can see that the hairs no longer cling together; the individual bristles are visible.

Why do the hairs cling together when wet and in air but not when immersed in water? How is this related to the fact that fish cannot live in air even though the concentration of oxygen in air is about six times its concentration in water?

Puzzler 15: Humans, Fish, and a Water-Oxygen-Air Math Puzzler

Air is about 20 percent oxygen. The solubility of oxygen in water is about 0.04 g/L at 20°C. Given that a mole (6 × 10^{23} molecules) of air weighs 28.8 g and occupies 24 L at 20°C and normal sea-level air pressure, show that the concentration of oxygen in air is about six times its concentration in water.

CAPILLARITY, EVAPORATION, MELTING, AND BOILING

All of us have used a cloth towel to dry ourselves after a bath or shower or a paper towel to clean up a spilled liquid or to dry a dish. But have you ever wondered what enables a towel to absorb water? If you look closely at a piece of paper towel under a microscope, you'll see that it is made of thousands of tiny wood fibers that lie very close to one another. Perhaps it is the very narrow spaces between or inside the fibers that "pulls" water into the towel. The next investigation will allow you to find out whether water does or does not move into narrow spaces.

Investigation 27: Capillarity

MATERIALS NEEDED

- Clear soda straw • Clear glass or plastic tumbler • Water and food coloring • Straws of different diameters and/or capillary tubes
- Two glass plates such as windowpanes • Large, wide rubber band
- Thin piece of wood • Large shallow container • Graph paper

Place a clear soda straw in a glass of colored water. If you look closely, you'll see that the water level inside the straw is higher than the level of the water outside. Now try using a narrower straw (one with a smaller diameter) or a clear hollow cocktail straw. If possible, borrow a few capillary tubes from your school's laboratory. Place these narrow tubes in water. Does water move into the tubes? If it does, is the height to which the water rises related to the tube's diameter?

To see how the height to which water rises in narrow spaces is affected by the width of the space, place a pair of glass plates in some shallow water to which food coloring has been added. **Ask an adult to help you** put a large wide rubber band around the glass plates to hold them (see Figure 24). **Wear gloves in handling the glass to prevent cuts on sharp edges**. Insert a thin strip of wood between the plates along one edge as shown. Then place the plates in a shallow container of colored water. Set the plates and water aside. You will look at them again at the end of this investigation.

The tendency of water (and other liquids) to "climb" up narrow spaces is called capillarity or capillary action. How is the height of the water in the space between the glass plates related to the width of the space?

Careful measurements of the inside diameter of a number of hollow glass tubes and the height to which water rises in the tubes can be made. Some data from one such experiment are given in Table 4. Use the data to plot a graph of the height to which the water rises (on the vertical axis) versus the diameter of the tube

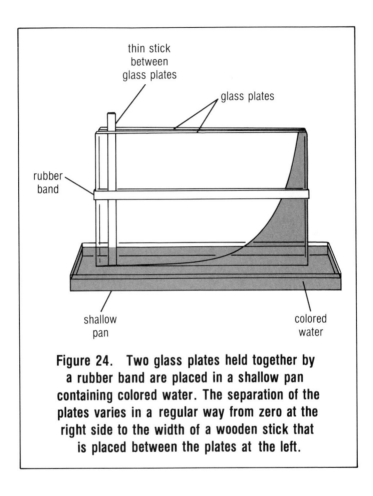

Figure 24. Two glass plates held together by a rubber band are placed in a shallow pan containing colored water. The separation of the plates varies in a regular way from zero at the right side to the width of a wooden stick that is placed between the plates at the left.

(on the horizontal axis). What does this graph suggest about the relationship between tube diameter and the height of the water in the tubes?

Next, plot a graph of the height to which water rises in the tubes versus the *inverse* of the tube diameter, that is, 1 over the diameter (1/diameter). Do you agree that this graph indicates that the height to which water rises in the tube is inversely proportional to the

TABLE 4: Data from an Experiment Comparing the Height to Which Water Rises in Glass Tubes with the Diameter of the Tubes.

Diameter of Tube (mm)	Height of Water in Tube (mm)
0.5	12
1.0	6
2.0	3
3.0	2
4.0	1.5

diameter of the tube? This is another way of saying that doubling the diameter of the tube halves the height to which water rises in the tube. Can you verify this with your own measurements?

How does the shape of the graph compare with the shape of the water between the glass plates that you placed in a shallow pan of water? How can you account for this?

CAPILLARITY: AN EXPLANATION

Capillarity is a rather common phenomenon. It occurs when ink enters blotting paper, when tea moves into a lump of sugar, when water rises between fine particles of soil, when melted candle wax moves up a wick, and when water is absorbed by a towel. But what is it that makes water move into small openings?

You've seen that there are strong cohesive forces holding water molecules together. But there are also adhesive forces that pull water toward glass, wood, cotton, wool, and other materials. For example, when you place drops of water on waxed paper they hold together better (spread out less) than they do on glass or plastic wrap. This is because the attractive forces between water and wax are weaker than those between water and glass.

If a narrow glass tube is placed in water, the water is attracted to the glass and so it moves up the tube. Because of the strong cohesive forces between water molecules, the water that moves up the tube pulls the other water molecules below it up the tube as well. This continues until the weight of the water balances the upward pull due to water-glass adhesive forces.

The curvature of the water surface at the top of the column in the narrow tube indicates that the pressure below the water surface is less than the air pressure above the water column. The weight of the narrow column of water in the tube divided by the cross-sectional area of the tube equals the pressure difference across the water surface.

An explanation of the pressure difference is very difficult. An alternative, though less satisfactory, explanation is to consider the surface of the water at the top of the tube to be stretched by the weight of the column of water it supports. The force due to the surface tension of the water along the circumference of the tube at the top of water column, which is $2\pi rS$, balances the weight of the water, and the weight of the water is proportional to its volume—$\pi r^2 h$. How does this confirm the fact that the height of the water in a narrow tube is inversely proportional to the radius or diameter of the tube?

Investigation 28: Testing an Explanation

MATERIALS NEEDED
- Clear soda straw • Soapy water and alcohol
- Straws of different diameters and/or capillary tubes

If the liquid in a narrow tube is supported by the force due to surface tension (the stretched film of water at the top of the tube), what does this suggest about the height to which soapy water will rise in narrow tubes as compared to the height to which water will rise in a tube of the same diameter? How about alcohol as compared to water? (Check the surface tensions and densities of soapy water and alcohol before you answer this question.)

With the same tubes that you used for water, test your predictions using soapy water and alcohol. Be sure to clean and dry the tube thoroughly before each experiment. What do you find? Do your experiments confirm your predictions?

Puzzler 16: A Capillary Puzzler
Water will rise twice as high in a capillary tube that is 1 mm wide as it will in a tube that is 2 mm wide. Does this mean that the same *volume of water rises up the different width tubes?*

Investigation 29: Capillary in Paper Towels: Covered and Uncovered

MATERIALS NEEDED
- Paper towels or white blotter paper • Scissors • Shallow container
- Water and food coloring • Tape • Waxed paper or plastic wrap

Cut a paper towel strip that is about 4 cm wide and 50 cm long. Hang the strip so that its lower end dips into a shallow container of colored water. See Figure 25a. What is the maximum height to which the water rises in the paper towel? How long does it take?

Now repeat the experiment, but this time cover the sides of the paper towel strip with waxed paper or plastic wrap as shown in Figure 25b. Be sure the end of the strip is in the colored water. How high does the water rise now? How long does it take?

Why do you think the water rises higher and faster in the covered strip than it does in the uncovered strip? Do you think the water will rise higher in an uncovered paper-towel strip on a humid day or on a day when the air is very dry? If possible, test your prediction experimentally.

- About how high do you think soapy water will rise in a similar strip of uncovered paper towel? How about alcohol? Cooking oil? Try the experiment using these liquids with separate paper towel strips. Were your predictions correct?

Investigation 30: Evaporation and Evaporation Rates

MATERIALS NEEDED
- Paper towels and scissors • Water and food coloring
- Balance to weigh towels • Clock or watch

If you did the experiment in the last investigation with an uncovered paper-towel strip on a humid day and on a dry day, you probably found that the water rose higher on the humid day than on the dry day. On a dry

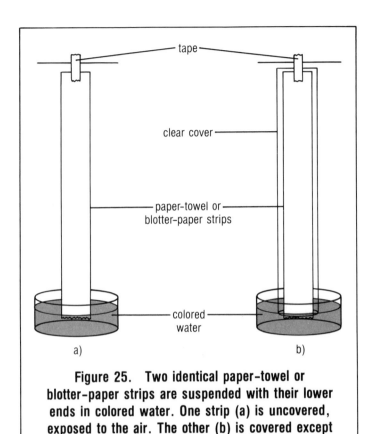

Figure 25. Two identical paper-towel or blotter-paper strips are suspended with their lower ends in colored water. One strip (a) is uncovered, exposed to the air. The other (b) is covered except along its lower edge, which is in water.

day, water evaporates rapidly from the paper towel as well as from other damp surfaces. But on a humid day there is already a lot of moisture in the air and so water moves into it less rapidly.

In this investigation you'll examine some other factors that affect the rate of evaporation. To begin, hang a dry paper towel from a balance as shown in Figure 26. How much does the towel weigh?

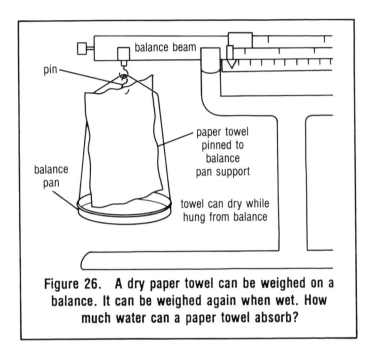

Figure 26. A dry paper towel can be weighed on a balance. It can be weighed again when wet. How much water can a paper towel absorb?

Now dip the towel in water, let the excess water flow out of the towel, and then weigh it again. How much water did the paper towel absorb? What happens to the mass of the wet paper towel as it hangs on the balance? Why?

Record the weight of the wet towel at 10-minute intervals for at least an hour. Then plot a graph of the towel's weight versus time. What happens to the rate at which water evaporates from the towel as time goes on?

• Design an experiment to find out how the area of the towel, which can be changed by folding it, affects the rate at which water evaporates.

- Design an experiment to find out how the temperature of the air affects the rate at which water evaporates from the towel.
- Design an experiment to find out how wind affects the rate at which water evaporates from the towel.

Investigation 31: Capillarity and Evaporation from Towels of Different Widths

MATERIALS NEEDED

- Paper towels or white blotter paper • Scissors and ruler • Water and food coloring • Long, shallow container • Tape

Prepare 50-cm long strips from paper towels or white blotter paper that have the following widths: 0.5 cm, 1.0 cm, 1.5 cm, 2.0 cm, 3.0 cm, and 4.0 cm. Do you think the width of the strips will affect the height to which water will rise in these strips when they are hung in the air without any covering?

Hang the strips side by side, about a centimeter apart, with their lower ends in a long shallow container of colored water. Examine the strips every few minutes until the water stops rising in all the strips. Does the water rise to the same height in each strip? If not, how do you explain the results you observe?

WHEN WATER CHANGES STATE

As you've seen, there are strong forces of attraction between water molecules. These forces play an important role in determining how much energy must be supplied to change water's state: that is, to convert it from a solid to a liquid or a liquid to a gas. In order to change a liquid to a gas, work must be done on the liquid molecules because they must acquire enough kinetic energy (move fast enough) to overcome the forces that hold them together and separate themselves from one another. Molecules are generally about ten times farther apart in the gaseous state than they are in the liquid state. Similarly, to break the bonds that hold the molecules of a solid in relatively fixed positions, energy must be supplied so that the molecules, although still in contact, are free to move about one another in the liquid state.

Puzzler 17: Change of State

The centers of molecules in the liquid state are about one diameter apart. When these molecules separate to form a gas, the distance between them increases to about ten molecular diameters. How does the volume occupied by the molecules of a gas compare with the volume occupied by the same molecules when they are in the gaseous state?

Investigation 32: Heat of Fusion

MATERIALS NEEDED
- Small plastic dish with a volume of about 200 mL
- Pill bottle or similar container with a volume of about 50 mL
- Strong rubber bands • Graduated cylinder • Freezer
- Thermometer • Basting syringe and eyedropper • Paper towel

You've seen that water freezes at 0°C (32°F). From earlier experiments, you probably realize that a mixture of water and ice remains at 0°C (32°F) as long as the freezing or melting process is taking place. For water to freeze, heat must be removed. Because this heat is associated with a loss of potential energy, not kinetic energy (the energy of motion), there is no temperature change during the process. Just as a ball falling to the floor loses gravitational potential energy, so water molecules, by forming ice crystals, acquire a lower potential energy level. Since the temperature remains at 0°C throughout the freezing process, there is no change in the kinetic energy of the molecules. Similarly, when ice melts, water molecules acquire additional potential energy. But since the water remains at 0°C throughout the melting process, there is no increase in the kinetic energy of the molecules.

How much energy is required to melt 1 gram of ice at the melting temperature (0°C)? You can find out by pouring water into a block of solid ice that has a cup-like hole in its center. To prepare such a block of ice, pour water into a plastic dish—one that holds about 200 mL of water. Place a large pill bottle or similar container with a volume of about 50 mL in the center of the water. Hold it in place with a pair of strong rubber bands as shown in Figure 27. Water should surround the cup, and there should be water below the cup as well. When the water has completely frozen (allow 12 hours), remove the rubber bands and the empty cup. Presto! you have a small block of ice with a hole in it. If you have trouble removing the cup, pour some warm water into it. The heat will melt the ice frozen to the cup so that you can easily remove it.

While you wait for the ice to reach 0°C (allow 5 minutes), measure out 30 to 35 mL of warm tap water.

Vast amounts of energy are required to melt a
glacier like this one in the Chigmit Mountains
of Alaska. Notice the icebergs being discharged
into the lake at the glacial margin.

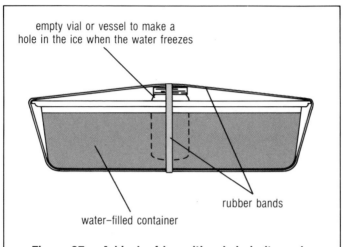

empty vial or vessel to make a
hole in the ice when the water freezes

rubber bands

water−filled container

**Figure 27. A block of ice with a hole in it can be
made by freezing water in a container like the one
shown. The rubber bands hold a vial in the water so
there will be a hole in the ice when the water freezes.**

Stir the water and record its temperature. Dry the hole
in the ice with a paper towel. Then carefully pour all
the warm water into the hole. Stir the water in the ice
until its temperature reaches the temperature of the ice
(0°C). Then use a basting syringe to remove the water
from the ice quickly and put it into a graduated cylinder. You may need a small syringe to remove the last
few drops. What is the volume of the water and melted
ice? How much ice melted?

The heat to melt this ice came from the warm
water as it cooled from its initial temperature down to
0°C. Suppose that you used 20 mL of water and that
its initial temperature was 40°C. In cooling from 40°

to $0°$ it lost 800 calories (20 g $\times$ 40°C) or 3300 J. (Remember, 1.0 J = 0.24 cal. or 4.2 J = 1.0 cal.) If you divide this heat by the mass of ice that melted, you will know how much heat is required to melt 1 gram of ice. This quantity of energy per gram is called the heat of fusion for ice.

Since energy is conserved, how much heat, according to your results, must be removed from a gram of water at 0°C to change it to ice at the same temperature?

Investigation 33: Another Experiment to Find the Heat of Fusion

MATERIALS NEEDED

• Graduated cylinder • Warm water • Insulated plastic foam cup • Ice cubes • Paper towels • Thermometer

Investigation 32 was easy conceptually because all the heat lost by the warm water was used to melt ice. However, its results may not be very accurate because there are a number of sources of error. What are they?

Assuming that room temperature is about 20°C, you may obtain better accuracy by doing the following: Place 100 mL (100 g) of warm tap water at about 30°C in an insulated plastic foam cup. Cool the water by adding ice until the water reaches 10°C. By cooling the water to a temperature that is about as many degrees below room temperature as it was above room temperature in the beginning, you can compensate for heat losses and gains during the experiment. That is, about as much heat will be lost by the warm water to the cooler surroundings (while the water cools from 30° to 20°) in the first part of the experiment as is gained from the warmer surroundings (while the water cools from 20° to 10°) during the second half of the experiment.

To do the experiment, use a paper towel to remove any cold water that may lie on the surface of an ice cube. (Why should you dry the ice?) Add the ice cube to the warm water and stir until all the ice has melted. If necessary, add another (dry) ice cube so that the final temperature of the ice is about 10°C. Then pour the water, to which the melted ice has now been added, into a graduated cylinder. How much ice melted?

The heat lost by the warm water can be found from the mass of the water (100 g) and its change in temperature. In the example given, the change in temperature of the warm water was 20°C (30°C − 10°C). Therefore, the warm water lost 2000 calories (100 g × 20°C) or 8400 J. However, in this experiment the heat lost by the water accomplished *two* things: (1) It melted the ice and (2) it warmed the melted ice from 0°C to the final temperature of the water.

Suppose that in the example given the final volume of water was 122 mL. Since 22 g (122 g − 100 g) of ice melted, the heat required to warm the melted ice was 220 cal (22 g × 10°C). The remaining 1780 calories (2000 − 220) must be the heat that was involved in melting the ice. Then according to these data the heat to melt 1 gram of ice was

$$\frac{1780 \text{ cal}}{22 \text{ g}} = 81 \text{ cal/g or } 340 \text{ J/g.}$$

How does this value compare with the one you found in your experiment?

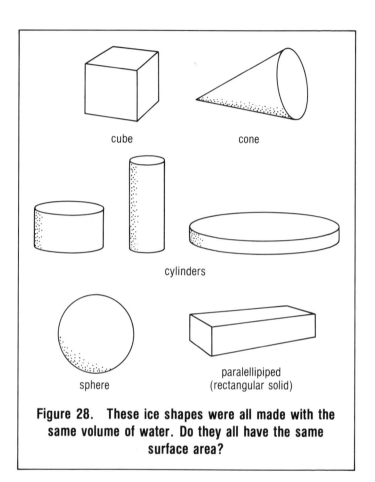

cube   cone

cylinders

sphere   paralellipiped
(rectangular solid)

Figure 28. These ice shapes were all made with the same volume of water. Do they all have the same surface area?

Puzzler 18: A Melting Rate Puzzler

The ice shapes shown in Figure 28 were all made with the same volume of water. Which piece of ice do you predict will melt slowest if placed in a bucket of water? Which piece will melt fastest? You might like to test your predictions by making and melting a similar set of ice shapes.

Puzzler 19: A Melting Ice Puzzler

Place an ice cube in a strainer above a sink. When the ice begins to melt, count the number of drops per minute that fall from the strainer. After the ice has nearly melted away, will the number of drops per minute become smaller or larger than before?

Puzzler 20: A Freezing Water Puzzler

Icicles often form when snow melts and drips off a roof. If it's warm enough to melt the snow, how can the melt water freeze to form icicles?

Puzzler 21: Another Freezing Water Puzzler

In late autumn or winter when a lake freezes, the ice forms first around the edges where water and land meet. Why then in the spring does the ice melt first around the edges where land and ice meet?

Investigation 34: Heat of Vaporization: A Rough Estimate

MATERIALS NEEDED

- 200-W immersion heater • 12- or 14-oz insulated foam plastic cups
- Beaker or can to support cups • Graduated cylinder • Thermometer
- Clock or watch with second hand or second mode • Safety goggles, long sleeves, and gloves

Since you will be working with household electricity and boiling water in this experiment, **work under adult supervision**. The heat required to boil away 1 gram of a liquid at its boiling point is called the heat of vaporization. As you know, the boiling point of water at sea level is 100°C, and the temperature of the water remains at this temperature throughout the boiling process. The energy added to the boiling water is used not to increase the temperature but rather to separate the molecules of water.

When an object is pulled farther from the earth, its gravitational potential energy increases. The raised object can do work if it loses energy by falling back to the earth. In a similar way, molecules of water acquire potential energy when they are separated. And they too lose energy as they go back together again in a process we call condensation.

To make a rough estimate of how much energy is required to change 1 gram of liquid water to gaseous water at the boiling point, you can use an immersion heater like the one you used before (Investigation 10) to boil away some water. (**Remember, never plug an immersion heater into an electrical outlet unless its coil is in water**.) If you know how much heat is used to boil away a certain mass of water, you can easily calculate the heat used in boiling away 1 gram.

Print on the immersion heater may say that it is a 200-W heater. The actual power of the heater, however, may be somewhat higher or lower. Therefore, the first thing you must do is calibrate the heater. You can do this by placing 200 g of cold water in a 12- or 14-oz insulated foam plastic cup. If possible, use water that is 5° to 10° cooler than the room. This will reduce the heat losses that occur when the water temperature rises above room temperature. (Stacking two or three such cups together will provide better insulation. Support the cups in a beaker or can.)

Place the immersion heater in the cold water and use a thermometer to measure the water temperature. Record the initial temperature of the water. Note and record the exact time you plug the immersion heater into an electrical outlet. Stir the water gently with the thermometer as the water is heated. After exactly 1 minute, grasp the *plug* (not the cord) and disconnect the heater. Leave the heater in the cup as you continue to stir the water to find its final temperature. Why should you leave the heater in the water after it is disconnected?

Record the water's final temperature and find its change in temperature. Then calculate the heat that the immersion heater transferred to the water in 1 minute. Repeat the experiment several times to be certain your results are consistent. How much heat does the immersion heater deliver in 1 minute? How much heat do you predict it will deliver in 30 seconds? Test your prediction. Were you right?

If the heater really delivers as much heat per second as its rating (200-W) indicates, it provides 200 J/s or 12,000 J/min (2870 cal/min). How does this value compare with the value you found by experiment?

Now place 150 mL (150 g) of cold tap water in a stack of insulated foam plastic cups. Support the cups with a beaker or can. When there is only 150 g of water, very little will spatter from the cup when the water boils! **However, as a matter of safety, wear**

goggles, long sleeves, and gloves throughout this experiment. Put the immersion heater into the water, stir, and record the initial temperature of the water. Plug in the heater and let it transfer heat to the water for 7 to 8 minutes. During that period a significant amount of water should boil away. Once the water is boiling, record its temperature. Why might it boil at some temperature other than 100°C?

After disconnecting the heater, remove it from the water and carefully, **while wearing gloves and safety goggles,** pour the hot water into a graduated cylinder. How much water remains? How much boiled away?

With the data you have collected, you can make an estimate of the amount of heat required to boil away 1 g of water at its boiling point. For example, suppose that your heater transfers 3000 cal/min to the water. In 8 minutes it will provide 24,000 cal. If the initial temperature of the water was 20°C and the boiling temperature was 100°C, then 12,000 calories (150 g × 80°C) was required to bring the water to the boiling point. Assume that the remaining 12,000 calories (24,000 − 12,000) was used to change liquid water to gaseous water. If 20 g of water boiled away, then the energy required to boil away 1 g of water was

$$\frac{12,000 \text{ cal}}{20 \text{ g}} = 600 \text{ cal/g}.$$

Using your data, what do you find is the heat of vaporization for water?

TABLE 5: Molecular Mass* and Heats of Vaporization and Fusion for a Number of Substances with Molecular Masses Reasonably Close to That of Water (18).

Substance	Molecular Mass (amu)	Heat of Vaporization (cal/g)	(J/g)	Heat of Fusion (cal/g)	(J/g)
Aluminum	27	2500	10,450	95	394
Ammonia	17	329	1370	108	453
Copper	63.5	1150	4790	49	205
Ethyl alcohol	46	205	855	26	109
Hydrogen	2	54	226	14	59
Methyl alcohol	32	282	1173	17	69
Oxygen	32	51	213	3	14
Water	18	540	2260	80	334

* In atomic mass units (amu).

Investigation 35: Heat of Vaporization: A Better Estimate

MATERIALS NEEDED

- 200-W immersion heater • 12- or 14-oz insulated foam plastic cups
- Pencil • Graduated cylinder • Thermometer • Clock or watch with second hand or second mode • Safety goggles, long sleeves, and gloves • Scissors • Rigid-board insulation (under cups) • Blanket-type insulation to surround cups

In the previous experiment you made a rough estimate of the heat of vaporization for water. The estimate was a rough one because the experiment involved a number of assumptions and errors. For example, you assumed that all the heat not used to raise the water's temperature to the boiling point went into changing the liquid to a gas. But, in fact, since the experiment was conducted at temperatures well above room temperature, a considerable amount of heat was lost to the surroundings. You assumed too that no water spattered away. What other errors were involved in that experiment?

You can reduce the experimental errors and obtain a more accurate value for the heat of vaporization of water by (1) providing more insulation around the water and heater and (2) covering the apparatus to eliminate spattering. Figure 29 shows the setup for this experiment.

If you did Investigation 34, there is no need to determine how much heat the immersion heater transfers per minute. If you didn't, go back and calibrate your heater as explained in that investigation.

Once you know how much heat the immersion heater transfers per minute, you can begin this experiment. Because you will be working with household electricity and boiling water, **work under adult supervision and wear safety goggles, long sleeves, and gloves throughout the experiment**. Stack one 12- or 14-oz insulated cup inside one or two others. Support them in a beaker or can. Then use a pair of scissors to cut off the rim of an identical cup. Use a pencil to punch a small hole through the bottom of the cup from inside to outside. The hole will allow steam to escape during the experiment. Pour 150 g of cold water into the stack of cups, and place the heater in the water. After measuring the initial temperature of the water, invert the rimless cup and slip it into the top of the cups that hold the water and heater. See Figure 29. It will cover the water and heater, reduce spattering, and provide better insulation. To reduce heat loss further, place the cups on a slab of rigid-board insulation and wrap a blanket of insulation around the sides of the insulated

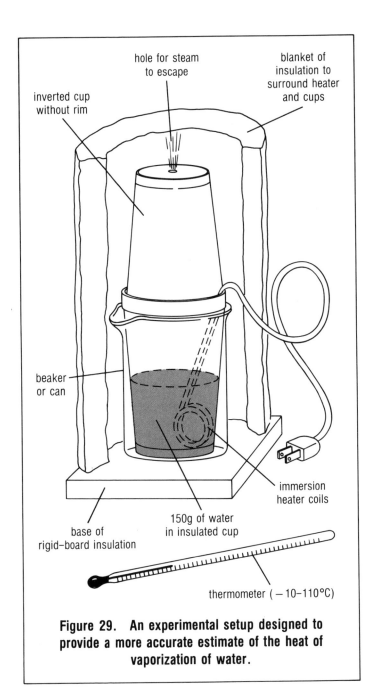

Figure 29.   An experimental setup designed to
provide a more accurate estimate of the heat of
vaporization of water.

foam plastic cups. The cord from the heater can emerge through the region where the blanket overlaps. Be sure you do not cover the opening at the top where steam will emerge.

Note the exact time, plug in the heater, and let the heater operate for 8 minutes. At the end of that time, disconnect the heater, remove it and the insulation from around the cups, and quickly pour the water into a graduated cylinder. How much of the 150 g of water remains? How much water boiled away?

How much heat was transferred to the water in 8 minutes? How much of that heat was required to raise the temperature of the cold water to the boiling point? Assuming no heat was lost to the surroundings, how much heat was used to boil away water? What is the heat of vaporization of water, in calories per gram (cal/ g) and joules per gram (J/g), according to your data?

Since the materials in this experiment were well insulated, it's reasonable to assume that less heat was lost to the surroundings in this experiment than in the previous one. However, undoubtedly some heat "leaked" away. What could you do to eliminate or take into account the small heat losses that occurred in this experiment? How can you obtain a still more accurate value for the heat of vaporization? If you design an experiment to find this value, be sure you **work under adult supervision.**

Investigation 36: Heat of Condensation

MATERIALS NEEDED
- Steam generator • Ring stand • Bunsen burner and tubing
- Matches • Rubber or plastic tubing • Wide, thick board

- Large test tube with two-hole rubber stopper • Glass tubing
- Eyedropper • 6- or 7-oz foam plastic cups • Thermometer
- Balance

In the last two experiments you measured the quantity of energy absorbed in boiling away 1 gram of water. The law of conservation of energy would suggest that the same quantity of energy would be released when a gram of steam condenses back to liquid water. To find out whether this is indeed the case, you can let some steam condense in cold water and see (1) whether energy is released and (2) whether the energy released per gram has the same numerical value as the heat of vaporization.

Figure 30 shows the setup for such an experiment. **Be careful! Steam can cause severe burns.** Because you'll be using a burner and working with steam, **be sure you work under the supervision of a qualified adult.** Steam produced in a generator flows through a rubber or plastic tube to a steam trap where water droplets carried by the steam are removed. The steam coming out of the trap travels along an insulated glass tube to an eyedropper. Scissors can be used to cut strips of insulation from a foam plastic cup that can then be wrapped around the glass tubing. The insulation can be held in place with rubber bands. The end of the eyedropper is immersed in cold water where the emerging steam condenses and warms the water.

To do the experiment, pour some water into the steam generator. If you don't have such a generator, you can use a Pyrex flask with a one-hole rubber stopper and a glass tube as shown in the Figure 30 insert. While the water is heating, use scissors to cut away the

131

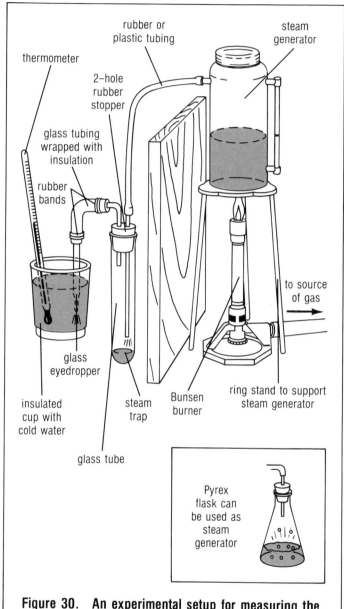

Figure 30. An experimental setup for measuring the heat of condensation of water.

top third of a 6- or 7-oz insulated foam plastic cup. Weigh the cup on the balance. Record its mass, fill it about three-fourths of the way with cold water (at about 10°C, or 10° below room temperature), and weigh it again. What is the mass of the cold water?

When dry steam (steam without water droplets) is emerging from the eyedropper, use the thermometer to measure the temperature of the cold water. Record this temperature. Then, **wearing safety glasses and gloves,** hold the cup of cold water so that the end of the eyedropper is beneath the water's surface. You'll hear the steam sputter as it condenses in the cold water. Stir the water gently with the thermometer. When the water temperature reaches 30°C, or a temperature about 10° greater than room temperature, remove the cup from the steam. Stir and record the water's maximum temperature.

Turn off the steam generator and determine the mass of the cup, water, and condensed steam. What mass of steam condensed? What is the purpose of starting with water colder than the room and allowing its temperature to rise to a level warmer than the room?

How much heat was transferred to the cold water? How much heat was released by the steam as it condensed? Don't forget to subtract out the heat that came from the hot water after it condensed. For example, if 5 g of steam condensed and the final temperature of the water was 30°C, the 5 g of condensed steam gave up 350 cal (1460 J) in cooling from 100°C down to 30°C (5 g × 70°C).

What is the heat of condensation for water according to your data? That is, how much heat is released when 1 gram of water vapor condenses to liquid at the boiling point?

Examine the heat of fusion and vaporization for a number of substances listed in Table 5. How does the energy required to separate the atoms of a metal compare with that required to separate the molecules of liquids? How does the heat of vaporization for water compare with that for other liquids and gases whose molecules have similar masses? On the basis of other experiments you have done, how might you explain water's rather extraordinary heat of vaporization?

ANSWERS
TO
PUZZLERS

1. The cube would be 1110 kilometers (690 miles) on a side.

2.

Name of Scale	Melting Point	Boiling Point
Celsius	0°	100°
Fahrenheit	32°	212°
Kelvin (Absolute)	273	373
Rankine	492°	672°

3. Add a drop of milk to a glass of water. Pour that water into a bottle that holds three glasses of water. Mix the diluted milk solution and remove one glassful. It will contain one-quarter drop of milk. A similar procedure can be used to obtain 1/100 drop of milk or 1/100 teaspoon of salt.

4. Invert the glass under water. Then use a flexible straw to blow or pump air into the glass. The air will displace the water from the glass.

5. To find the volume of sand *and* the air between the sand particles, pour some sand into a dry graduated cylinder and

measure the volume (V_{s+a}). Pour the dry sand into a beaker. Then pour some water into the empty graduated cylinder. Note the volume of the water (V_w). Pour the sand back into the water and measure the volume of the sand and water (V_{s+w}). The volume of the sand particles, (V_s), is $(V_{s+w}) - (V_w)$. The volume of the air between the particles is $(V_{s+a}) - (V_s)$. How can you find what percentage of the space filled by sand is really air?

6. Place one of the stirrers next to the seam where the two water-filled vessels meet. By blowing air into the seam, air bubbles will form in the water. These bubbles will rise to the top of the inverted plastic cup, forcing water out the seam and into the empty container below.

7. Your finger displaces some water. As far as the balance is concerned, you have added the water displaced to the container and so that side becomes heavier than the other side.

8. Even though the law of conservation of mass tells us that the mass will not change, the mass will *appear to* decrease. As the volume of the bag increases, it displaces more air. Therefore, the buoyant force on the bag increases, reducing the force with which the bag pulls on the balance beam.

9. Put the piece of paper towel over the mouth of the vial or tube. You can then invert the tube and the water will not flow out. Air pressure at the base of the tube exerts a force that will counteract the gravitational force on the water. You can then lower the inverted tube into the dish of water.

10. Not very well because air goes through the hole in the straw and into your mouth. This prevents you from reducing the pressure in your mouth so that air pressure on the water can force it up the straw the way it normally does.

11. When you draw water into the straw, the volume of gas above the liquid in the sealed bottle increases. This reduces the pressure of the gas. Less pressure means a smaller force pushing the liquid up the straw.

12. Tap the top vessel gently with the spoon to form a narrow, crescent-shaped opening where the vessels meet. Surface tension will prevent the water from flowing out. Drop the dime through the opening.

13. Place a drop of water at the center of the star. The forces of surface tension will pull the toothpicks together to form a five-point star.

14. The forces of surface tension draw the hairs together, but if the brush is in water these forces act in all directions, outward as well as inward, so the hairs remain apart.

The gills of a fish, like the hairs of a brush, will stick together in air. This greatly reduces the area of contact between the air and the blood vessels in the gills.

15. The density of air is (28.8 g/24 L) = 1.2 g/L. Since 20 percent of the air is oxygen, 1.2 g/L $\times$ 0.20 = 0.24 g/L. 0.24 g/L/0.04 g/L = 6.

16. No! Using the data in Table 4, we see that the water rises to a height of 6 mm in a tube 1 mm wide and 3 mm high in a tube 2 mm wide. Assume the tubes are square. The volume of water in the 1-mm-wide tube is 1 mm $\times$ 1 mm $\times$ 6 mm = 6 mm^3. The volume of water in the 2 mm-wide tube is 2 mm $\times$ 2 mm $\times$ 3 mm = 12 mm^3. The tube that is twice as wide holds twice as much water.

Show that this holds true for a circular tube as well. Why should a tube twice as wide be able to support twice as much water?

17. The volume of a gas is about 1000 times that of the liquid from which it comes. If the molecules are ten times as far apart, then the three-dimensional space they occupy is 1000 times greater: 10 $\times$ 10 $\times$ 10.

18. The piece with the least surface area (the sphere) will melt slowest. The piece with the greatest surface area will melt fastest. The rate of heat flow is proportional to surface area.

19. The number of drops per minute will decrease as the ice cube melts because the surface area through which heat enters the ice also decreases as the ice shrinks in size.

20. Heat from the sun or heat coming through the roof may increase the temperature on the roof above the freezing point. If the temperature of the air and shingles at the edge of the roof is below the freezing point, the water will freeze again, forming icicles.

21. It takes much more heat to change the temperature of water than it does to change the temperature of an equal amount of soil; therefore, soil cools and warms much faster than water.

FOR
FURTHER
READING

Brown, Bob. *More Science for You: 112 Illustrated Experiments*. Blue Ridge Summit, Pa.: TAB Books, 1988.

Dolan, Edward F. *Drought: The Past, Present, and Future Enemy*. New York: Watts, 1990.

Gardner, Robert. *Water: The Life Sustaining Resource*. New York: Messner, 1982.

Goldin, Augusta. *Water: Too Much, Too Little, Too Polluted?* San Diego: Harcourt, 1983.

Herbert, Don. *Mr. Wizard's Supermarket Science*. New York: Random House, 1980.

Milne, Antony. *Our Drowning World*. Houston: Prism Press, 1988.

Niering, William A. *Wetlands*. New York: Knopf, 1985.

Palmer, Joy. *The World's Water*. United Kingdom: Batsford, 1988.

Pringle, Laurence. *Water: The Next Great Resource Battle*. New York: Macmillan, 1982.

VanCleave, Janice Pratt. *Chemistry for Every Kid.* New York: Wiley, 1989.

Watson, Lyall. *The Water Planet: A Celebration of the Wonder of Water*. New York: Crown, 1988.

INDEX